The Blessed Damozel

The University of North Carolina Press, Chapel Hill, N. C.; The Baker and Taylor Company, New York; Oxford University Press, London; Maruzen-Kabushiki-Kaisha, Tokyo; Edward Evans & Sons, Ltd., Shanghai; D. B. Centen's Wetenschappelijke Boekhandel, Amsterdam.

THIS EDITION IS LIMITED TO FOUR HUNDRED COPIES, AND THE TYPE FROM WHICH IT WAS PRINTED HAS BEEN MELTED.

DANTE GABRIEL ROSSETTI

The Blessed Damozel

THE UNPUBLISHED MANUSCRIPT
TEXTS AND COLLATION

WITH AN

INTRODUCTION

BY

PAULL FRANKLIN BAUM

CHAPEL HILL
THE UNIVERSITY OF NORTH CAROLINA PRESS
1937

Copyright, 1937, by
The University of North Carolina Press

CONTENTS

INTRODUCTION
pages ix-lvi

THE BLESSED DAMSEL, 1847
(from the manuscript)
pages 5-9

THE BLESSED DAMOZEL, 1850
(from *The Germ*)
pages 11-16

THE BLESSED DAMOZEL, 1856
(from *The Oxford and Cambridge Magazine*)
pages 17-21

THE BLESSED DAMOZEL, 1881
(with variant readings)
pages 23-30

NOTE

I am greatly indebted to Miss Belle da Costa Greene, Director of the Pierpont Morgan Library, New York City, for permission to print, for the first time, the only known manuscript version of 'The Blessed Damozel.'

I wish to thank also Mr. Frederick Page for the use of his collations of the poem, and particularly for the details from the two Trial Books of 1869 and the proof-sheets of 1870 (which I have not seen).

P. F. B.

INTRODUCTION

I

'The Blessed Damozel' exists now in four principal versions. The first, 1847, in the Morgan manuscript, comprises twenty stanzas in the same order as the final version, save that stanza xi follows stanza xvi;[1] the second, 1850, in *The Germ*, adds six stanzas (vi, vi*a*, xvii*a*, xvii*b*, xx, xxii*a*) and omits one (xi); the third, 1856, in *The Oxford and Cambridge Magazine*, restores stanza xi (in its original position) and retains only two (vi, xx) of the six added in 1850; the fourth, in the *Poems*, 1870, transfers stanza xi to its final position, with no other changes in arrangement. After 1870 there were a few alterations in single passages. The 1850 version is thus the most 'peculiar' of the four, inasmuch as it contains four stanzas afterwards cancelled and omits the significant stanza xi, to say nothing of many variants of detail which were later rejected.

That the first version was composed by 1847 is quite certain. In a letter (printed without date) Rossetti wrote to Hall Caine: "... *The Blessed Damozel*, which I wrote (and have altered little since) when I was eighteen. It was first printed when I was twenty-one."[2] He was eighteen between 12 May 1846 and 12 May 1847. In *Rossetti as Designer and Writer* (pp. 125 f.) William Michael Rossetti, citing a letter of 1873 (to be mentioned again), tells us that the poem was written with a view to its in-

---

[1] The line and stanza numbering is that of the final version.

[2] This letter must have been written between 29 July 1879 (the date of Rossetti's first letter to Hall Caine) and July 1881, when Caine "took up his regular abode" in the Cheyne Walk house (William Michael Rossetti, *Dante Gabriel Rossetti: His Family-Letters with a Memoir*, London, 1895, 1, 369; cited hereafter as *L. and M.*). This letter appears to be the basis of W. M. R.'s statements in *Rossetti as Designer and Writer*, 1889, and in the *Memoir*, *L. and M.*, I, 107.

THE BLESSED DAMOZEL

sertion in the "manuscript family-magazine named Hodgepodge, which was concocted, never passing beyond the range of the family circle, during some months or weeks of 1847, or possibly 1846."[3] Moreover, with a letter dated 25 November 1847 Rossetti sent 'The Blessed Damozel' to William Bell Scott among his then projected collection of "Songs of the Art Catholic."[4]

The Morgan manuscript, however, though signed "D. G. R. 1847," was clearly not written in 1847—for two reasons. First, in 1847 the poet had not changed his baptismal name of Gabriel Charles Dante Rossetti to the now familiar Dante Gabriel Rossetti. The early letters are signed "Gabriel C. Rossetti," "Gabriel Rossetti," "G. Rossetti," "Gabriel C. D. Rossetti," "Gabriel Chas. Rossetti," "G. C. Rossetti," "Gabriel Dante Rossetti" down to 1849.[5] The second reason is that the handwriting is not that of the early letters and manuscripts. Sir Sidney Cockerell[6] estimates the script of the Morgan manuscript as "perhaps ten years later" than 1847, noting that the round capital A of the early letters persisted in Rossetti's writing at least as late as 1852. I should like to suggest an even later date, with which I think the script would equally well agree.

In a letter to his mother from Kelmscott, 20 May 1873, Rossetti says:

I remember that for the family Hotch Potch, long and long ago, I first wrote *The Blessed Damozel,* and also a poem about a portrait. Have you these ancient documents, and could you let me have the same if in my own handwriting? . . . What is the date thereof?[7]

---

[3] This magazine seems to have completely disappeared now. Diligent inquiry in many directions has failed to uncover any trace of it.

[4] Scott's *Autobiographical Notes,* London, 1890, I, 243 ff.

[5] Cf. *L. and M.,* II, 47; and K. L. Knickerbocker ("Rossetti's 'The Blessed Damozel,'" in *Studies in Philology,* XXIX (1932), 485-504), p. 496, n. 39.

[6] In a letter to Miss Greene, 7 February 1933.

[7] *L. and M.,* II, 293.

The date here is interesting, for it was in 1873 that Rossetti began his drawings for pictures of 'The Blessed Damozel.'[8] Obviously his mind was much occupied with the idea of the Blessed Damozel, and naturally turned back to the earliest composition of the poem. It would be characteristic of him to try to recover some of the first inspiration by seeing his old manuscript and thus reviving old memories. Perhaps—though this is of course merely a conjecture—his mother sent him a copy of the Hotch Potch, or some early draft of the poem, from which he made a fair copy in 1873, and the Morgan manuscript is that copy. The manuscript is certainly a fair copy; for the few corrections are such as spring from miswriting rather than revision.

THE BLESSED DAMOZEL

The frequent similarities between this 1847 version and that of 1856 might raise a suspicion that it is not an exact copy of the text as it stood before 1850. Yet the special peculiarities of *The Germ* version, with its many discarded alterations, would appear to indicate that Rossetti was in a mood for free emendation when he prepared the version of 1850; and in any event, the fact that he restored in 1856 many readings of 1847 cannot be held to militate against the date which he set on the manuscript.

I propose now to examine the earliest form of the poem, that of the Morgan manuscript. Probably no poem ever written is so ill-suited to a prose paraphrase as this one; yet I shall venture a descriptive analysis of it, somewhat in the manner of Dante's *divisione*. A poem which does not possess enough substance to bear a sympathetic examination is hardly worth reading at all.

In the first two stanzas we see the blessed damsel leaning against the bar of heaven, clothed in the simple white of one

[8] *Rossetti as Designer and Writer*, p. 86; Marillier, who also mentions a letter of May 1873 to Madox Brown referring to a crayon of this subject.

THE BLESSED DAMOZEL devoted to the service of the Virgin. This picture is elaborated with three descriptive touches, each of a different import. The third and simplest is her hair "lying down her back," "yellow like ripe corn"; a purely visual image emphasizing her appearance in heaven as she had been on earth. The second is part visual and part symbolic—the lilies in her hand and the stars in her hair. The first describes the quiet depth of her dark eyes, which is further explained in the next stanza: although she had been ten years in heaven, the time seemed to her but a day and her eyes still showed her wonderment at being there. The irregular order in which these details are given us is interesting and is characteristic of the deliberate simplicity of the whole poem. The picture is built up with an apparent carelessness and lack of arrangement which enhance our sense of its reality.

In the next stanza we are suddenly transported to the earth, where her lover fancies that the autumn leaves are her hair about his face. (This is sometimes referred to as his 'vision.') The poem at once becomes dramatic; and the contrast intensifies both pictures.

Then we are shown in successive stanzas, following the same unsystematic arrangement of details, the infinite distance separating the two; we have, for background, a glimpse of her companions at play; we see the blessed damsel again, apart from her friends, still leaning intently above the infinite space, searching for the little world in which her lover still waits. And this general picture is still further elaborated with two images which rather confuse than assist the imagination: the souls of the dead rising to heaven "like thin flames," and the "vast waste calm" of space filled with the fierce pulsation of Time. Surely it seems as though the poet (as the painter afterwards in his drawings and paintings) was concerned to crowd every inch of his picture with details, heedless of the danger of distracting our attention from the main subject. Yet these apparently irrelevant and disturbing images contribute somehow to the whole effect, as though the picture, being remote from our ordinary experience, could be better realized by confusion than by clarity.

THE BLESSED DAMOZEL

Then through nine stanzas (interrupted once, after the fifth) we hear the blessed damsel speaking. Her voice sounds—again an image that will not fuse with what preceded—like the sweetness of the music of the spheres.—"I am certain that he will come to me," she says, "and then we shall go hand in hand to God's throne, we shall lie together under the Tree of Life, and I shall tell him about the mysteries of Heaven. . . . We shall go to Mary, whose handmaidens are weaving garments for those new-born into the heavenly life, and She will take us to Christ. I shall ask Him to let us live happily together as on earth."

Nothing could be more simple and childlike than this, or more poignantly tender. And in the midst of her speech, to heighten the poignancy, we see once more the lover on earth, who fancies he hears her voice in a bird's song and her footsteps, as she comes down to him, in the sound of bells,—just as he felt her hair in the autumn leaves.

The damsel paused; then said wistfully: "All this is when he comes." Angels flew past her in a gleam of light, and she smiled. When the angels were gone she laid her face on the bar of heaven and wept.

Is it surprising that Christina, with her intense religious fervor, should say that the poem "falls short of expressing the highest view"? It is true that Beatrice was in heaven while Dante was on earth; but could anything be less like Dante or Dante's Paradise than this heaven in which the damsel, withdrawing from the other blessed, thinks only of reunion with her earthly lover and weeps because he is not there?

THE BLESSED DAMOZEL

II

'The Blessed Damozel' was virtually complete in 1847.[9] The subsequent changes do not alter the significance or the characteristic beauty of the poem. Some of the changes in 1850 are of considerable interest however. The choice of *damozel* for *damsel* was a happy inspiration;[10] and the concomitant changes of "leaned out" for "against" and "gold" for "silver" are equally happy. The third and fourth lines were certainly not improved in 1850. Though the repetition of "robe" in line 9 from line 7 looks like a careless error, the "rose" worn on the neck (1850) is not altogether pleasing; and the first reading makes better sense and better grammar. "Terrace" for "rampart" is a good illustration of the infelicitous alterations of 1850; but on the other hand the new stanza vi, with its vivid images, is proof that Rossetti could perfectly well recover the feeling of the first draft.[11]

Stanza vi*a* points the contrast between the fretfulness of earth and the silent peace of heaven. No reason is apparent

---

[9] Dr. Knickerbocker takes a different view: "that the perfect round of the poem, either as to content or form, was not realized until many years after the poem was first conceived"; and he contrasts "its original ingenuous state" with "its later more sophisticated form."

[10] *Damozel* occurs in Spenser and in the King James Bible and was not uncommon in the sixteenth and seventeenth centuries. Rossetti himself used it more than once in his translations from the Early Italian Poets (e. g., in Cavalcanti's Ballata (viii), *The Works*, 1911, p. 360) which were mostly done before 1850, though revised later. On this word see also the remarks of Max Nordau, p. lii below.

[11] We have a glimpse of how the new stanzas multiplied in 1850 in W. M. R.'s P. R. B. Journal (*Praeraphaelite Diaries and Letters*, London, 1900, pp. 250 f.). Under 25 January this entry: "Gabriel finished up his *Blessed Damozel*, to which he added two stanzas." The next day: "Gabriel sent Tupper [the printer of *The Germ*] an additional stanza for *The Blessed Damozel*." And a little later: "Gabriel wrote one more stanza for his *Blessed Damozel*." In his introduction to an illustrated edition of the poem, London, 1898, W. M. R. says (p. viii): "Before publishing the poem in *The Germ*, my brother added four stanzas to it. I cannot say with any precision which they were; but I think they must have been stanzas 6, 9, 13, and either 14 or 17" that is, of the final version stanzas vi, viii, xiv, and either xv or xvii*b*. Actually, as we have seen, they were stanzas vi, vi*a*, xvii*a*, xvii*b*, xx, xxii.

why it should have been removed, unless perhaps there is a suggestion of inconsistency between the peace of heaven and the Damozel's longing for her lover.[12]

Very striking is the omission of stanza xi from the 1850 text. At first this stanza came at the end of the Damozel's speech (st. xiii-xvi) instead of, as finally, at the beginning. That is, the words of the lover on earth are heard in the fourth stanza and then only once again (except briefly at the end) just past the middle of the poem. In 1850, when two stanzas were added after this speech, the proportions remained the same, but the substituted stanzas, later cancelled, are as puzzling as the omission of xi. In this stanza, restored in 1856 along with a new one immediately following (xvii), the earthly lover thinks he hears the Damozel's voice in the song of a bird and her approaching footsteps in the sound of bells. We may assume however that Rossetti cancelled this stanza in 1850 because he felt that the two new ones were a preferable substitute.—

> (Alas! to *her* wise simple mind
>   These things were all but known
> Before: they trembled on her sense,—
>   Her voice had caught their tone.
> Alas for lonely Heaven! Alas
>   For life wrung out alone!
>
> Alas, and though the end were reached? . . . .
>   Was *thy* part understood
> Or borne in trust? And for her sake
>   Shall this too be found good?—
> May the close lips that knew not prayer
>   Praise ever, though they would?)

The reasons for rejecting them however in all the subsequent versions are not hard to see. The lover on earth has over-

[12] Dr. Knickerbocker is more positive. He believes it was omitted "because it contradicts an important idea in the poem as a whole. . . . The idea of heaven as a vacuum of silence clashes with such phrases as 'God's choristers,' 'angels . . . shall sing,' and the whole conception of heaven as an anticipatory state of spiritualized gossip."

THE BLESSED DAMOZEL

THE BLESSED DAMOZEL heard what the Damozel was saying in heaven (st. xiii-xvi) when she described their future union in paradise; she had already said much the same thing to him while she was alive; but he longs for her nonetheless. (The unconsciously anticipated biographical fact—that a dozen years later Elizabeth Siddal had become his blessed damozel—needs no comment.) And what is much more, he is distrustful of her prophecy now as he had been before. He is not sure that their union in heaven would be best for her. He has not been religious on earth: could he ever become so after death?—This complication, while adding a remarkable dramatic element to the whole situation, is so disconcerting as to interfere with the general tone of the poem. W. M. R. says similarly—after praising "Alas for lonely Heaven" as "one of the most moving audacities in the poem"—"This indicates past undevoutness in the lover, or perhaps even a certain degree of unbelief. Rossetti must eventually have considered it better to exclude any such idea."[13]

Another distinguishing mark of the 1850 text is the change in stanza xxii and the addition of a new stanza, afterwards rejected.

[xxii] "There will I ask of Christ the Lord
                Thus much for him and me:—
            To have more blessing than on earth
                In no wise; but to be
            As then we were,—being as then
                At peace. Yea, verily.

[xxii*a*] "Yea, verily; when he is come
                We will do thus and thus:
            Till this my vigil seem quite strange
                And almost fabulous;
            We two will live at once, one life;
                And peace shall be with us.

[13] Edition cited, 1898, pp. xii f. Again (p. xiii) he refers to this as "a certain sceptical tendency in the lover, a germ of disunion between himself and his beloved in matters of faith."

There is nothing new in this; the emphasis on "peace" is again unfortunate in its implication of disharmony on earth; the repetition of "Yea, verily" is ineffective (like the repetition of "Alas" in the other rejected stanzas); and the language is in general less felicitous than in the rest of the poem.[14]

Altogether, then, the revision of 1850 was not entirely satisfactory. That this was recognized as so is evident from Rossetti's changes when he published 'The Blessed Damozel' in *The Oxford and Cambridge Magazine* six years later. The circulation of *The Germ* had been so limited that he could have had no hesitation in reprinting; and the opportunity for revision must have been welcome. Four of the six new stanzas of 1850 he discarded entire (vi*a*, xvii*a*, xvii*b*, xxii*a*), and he contributed two new ones. The first of these, stanza x, cannot be said to be a quite happy addition, although Rossetti allowed it to stand. It has the pretty figure of "the curled moon . . . like a little feather Fluttering far down the gulf"; but the going of the sun suggests earth rather than heaven, and the sun moreover was scarcely visible from "the ramparts of God's house" (st. v). The remainder of the stanza is mere repetition of the last two lines of the preceding stanza—to say nothing of the obvious rime-word "weather."

The other new stanza (xvii) follows the restored stanza xi and displaces the rejected xvii*a*, xvii*b*. There are thus two adjacent stanzas depicting the lover's feelings on earth, that in which he seems to hear her voice in the bird's song and her footsteps in the sound of bells, and the new one in which he echoes her "We two, we two," and doubts whether God will unite them because of his unworthiness. This last modification of the "past undevoutedness in the lover" is a clear improvement.

[14] Dr. Knickerbocker notes: "The jingling sort of rhythm, the indirection and meaninglessness of the second line [of st. xxii*a*] were enough to cause the elimination of the whole stanza."

THE BLESSED DAMOZEL   The principal change in the version of 1870 is the shift of stanza xi to a place after stanza x, separating the two parenthesized stanzas of the 1856 text and so distributing more evenly throughout the whole poem the indications of the earthly lover's presence: first, in the midst of the descriptive stanzas at the beginning; then just before the group of five stanzas (xii-xvi) containing her first soliloquy, and following this, just before the five stanzas (xviii-xxii) of her second soliloquy; and finally, in half lines at the very end. The virtue of this arrangement is plain, though it was reached only after some effort. The poem has ultimately achieved structure along with its other qualities.

One special kind of revision, to which I have already alluded in a parenthesis, is dwelt upon by Dr. Knickerbocker and calls for fuller discussion: the "subtle and successive revisions" by which Rossetti has "coloured the texture of the poem with biographical touches." It must be remembered, says Dr. Knickerbocker, that the Damozel herself, "who had been a boy's conception originally, had passed into the beautiful reality of Elizabeth Siddal by 1856, and had then been metamorphosed into a conscience-stricken dream of a guiltless and wronged wife by 1869." The contrast, in stanzas vi, vi*a*, of the peace of heaven to the restlessness of this world might be a part of this evolution; but vi*a* appeared only in the 1850 text. A similar emphasis on peace occurred in stanzas xxii and xxii*a*. But xxii*a* appeared likewise only in the 1850 text; and though "At peace" was retained in stanza xxii in 1856, it is still difficult to find any real biographical bearing in the phrase. Dr. Knickerbocker instances the cancelled stanzas xvii*a*, xvii*b* of 1850 and the substitution for them in 1869 (actually in 1870) of the present stanza xvii as evidence of Rossetti's weaving into the imaginary story of the Damozel reminiscences of his own wife; but these changes I shall try to explain differently on a later page, and at best stanza xvii need only suggest the conventional idea of the lover's unworthiness.

It is, however, on stanza xi that Dr. Knickerbocker rests his case. When in 1856 stanzas xvii*a* and xvii*b* of the 1850 text were omitted, they were replaced by transposing stanza xi (which occurred in the earliest version) to follow stanza xvi. "As such, these verses have very little significance except as expressing a healthy and somewhat blithe occultism. Thirteen years later, however, they whispered through an unhealthy mind—a mind tainted by sleeping potions, whisky, and haunting memories—and played it a fantastic trick." Dr. Knickerbocker now relates (from Mr. Waugh rather than from William Bell Scott, who is our authority for it) the familiar story of Rossetti's finding a tame bird in his path one day at Penkill (in 1868) and exclaiming: "It is my wife, the spirit of my wife, the soul of her has taken this shape; something is going to happen to me." Stanza xi, continues Dr. Knickerbocker, "must have been linked by Rossetti with this incident. And does not this event find poignant expression in the revision of the last three and a half lines of this stanza, now made to read:

> When those bells
> Possess'd the mid-day air,
> *Strove not her steps to reach my side*
> Down all the echoing stair?

And does not the preceding stanza, included now for the first time, take on a significance even greater than the remarkable simile it contains?—

> *The sun was gone now;* the curled moon
> Was like a little feather
> Fluttering far down the gulf; *and now*
> She spoke through the still weather.
> Her voice was like the voice the stars
> Had when they sang together.

THE BLESSED DAMOZEL

In fact, as it appears to us, this poem which had its inception as a form of poetic exercise, had by 1869 become freighted with biographical details." It is not clear what Dr. Knickerbocker means by "included now for the first time," since stanza x appeared first in 1856, not in 1869 or 1870. And the argument is somewhat weakened moreover by the fact that the chaffinch incident occurred in 1868, whereas the line

> Was she not stepping to my side

remained unaltered through the two Trial Books of 1869 and was changed to

> Strove not her steps to reach my side

only in the proof copy of the 1870 *Poems*. More than a year elapsed, with two printed texts, between the incident and the revision. And "those bells" (l. 63) to which Dr. Knickerbocker atttached great importance in connection with the incident of the castle bell, also related by Scott, appear in the earliest text of the poem.

Two explanations are possible. One may find in the general parallel between the early poems and the later biographical fact a curious instance of that unconscious prophecy of Rossetti's noted by Mr. Mégroz apropos of the *bout-rimés* sonnets;[15] or one may assume, with Dr. Knickerbocker, that the revision in 1870 was influenced—perhaps even consciously—by the memory of the chaffinch incident of 1868. Certainly the memory of this incident would give additional, if not exaggerated, importance to the similar situations; and it is as certain as such a thing can be without documentary evidence, that in 1869 or 1870 Rossetti recognized the likeness between his imaginary lover of 1847 looking up towards the Blessed Damozel and himself thinking of Lizzie Siddal's "soul-seques-

[15] R. L. Mégroz, *Dante Gabriel Rossetti: Painter Poet of Heaven in Earth*, London, 1928, p.185; and *The Works*, 1911, pp. 263 ff.

tered face Far off." A poet's gift is not necessary in order to perceive the poignancy (and the irony) of such a parallel.

III

It remains now to notice the more important of the alterations of detail—attempts to smoothe out the metre and to perfect the phrasing. Opinions will differ of course on the success of many of these revisions; and while we are bound to respect the poet's final judgment to the fullest degree, we may remember that Rossetti is almost notorious for retouching and repainting his pictures with frequently disastrous results. There is the word of so competent a critic as Swinburne that in this poem "the changes introduced were almost invariably for the better"; but this is a qualified statement and itself subject to interpretation. Moreover, there is in these various readings a special interest as a study of the poet's search for perfection. Rarely do we find so large a body of detailed revisions enabling us to observe a part of the poetic process.

Only one stanza was allowed to remain through all the versions unaltered, xviii. In stanzas iii and x the changes were trifling. For the rest, there are substantial variants throughout. I begin with the slighter ones and proceed to the more complex.[1]

The reading "robe" in line 9 is unmistakable in the Morgan manuscript; but though the grammar is loose there is no difficulty. The substitution of "rose" in 1850 brought with it a new line 10:

On the neck neatly worn;—

[1] These revisions have been already considered most fully by W. M. R. in the Introduction to his separate edition, 1898, already mentioned; and by K. L. Knickerbocker in the article cited above, p. x, note 5. A partial and inaccurate table of variants appeared in William Sharp's *Dante Gabriel Rossetti. A Record and a Study*, London, 1882. A fuller list was given in the Mosher edition, Portland, Maine, 1901. Cf. also R. L. Tyrrell, "Revision of 'The Blessed Damozel,'" in *The Academy*, LXX (1904), 356.

THE BLESSED DAMOZEL and doubtless the picture seemed unsatisfactory. Then the two readings were combined, giving a somewhat uncertain effect, since it is not clear why a white rose should be suitable "for service." The next line stood:

> And her hair lying down her back

until the proof copy of 1870.[2] The revision:

> Her hair that lay along her back

is smoother metrically, and for this reason perhaps weaker. Dr. Knickerbocker calls it "regular to the point of rippling—an excellent quality for hair."

In stanza v the three principal changes were temporary; they appeared in 1850 and were thereafter dropped and the readings of 1847 restored. So also the two in stanza xii; "tremble" for "are stirred" in stanza xiv, and the rewriting of the last two lines of this stanza with a better rime but inferior sense; the inversions in stanzas xv, xx; the three changes in stanza xvi; and "Amid the poised" for "in distant" in stanza xxiv.

"Darkness" (l.34) is a manifest improvement over "blackness" in 1850 and 1856. Again, the change of line 45 from

> Till her bosom's pressure must have made

in 1847 and 1850 to

> Until her bosom must have made

is a sacrifice to metrical smoothness. And the same may be said for the successive "Within that gulf" in 1847—"In that steep gulph" 1850—"Within the gulf" 1856 et seqq. Similar though more complex is the series: "We will step down as to a stream" 1847—"And we will . . ." 1850, 1856—"We will . . ." 1870-1873; but the final inversion

> As unto a stream we will step down

is just right.

[2] Rossetti to his brother, 27 August 1869: "Is the sound awkward? Is 'And her hair laid upon' etc. better?" (*L. and M.*, II, 208).

Line 49 presented a difficulty. From 1847 to 1856 it remained "the fixed lull of Heaven"—"lull" for contrast between the tumult of the world and the silent peace (especially in stanza vi*a*) of heaven; "fixed" for contrast between the fierce pulsing of Time and the steadiness of Heaven. "Fixed place" was Rossetti's best solution. It may seem a bit weak, but it was permitted to stand.

A good example of gradual and subtle improvement may be seen in line 61: "Alas! just now" 1847—"Ah sweet! Just now" 1856-1870[a]—"Ah sweet! Even now" 1870. But on the other hand tastes will differ as to the three versions of lines 109, 110:

> They sit in circle, with bound locks
>   And brows engarlanded;   1847
> Circle-wise sit they, with bound locks
>   And bosoms covered;   1850
> Circlewise sit they, with bound locks
>   And foreheads garlanded;   1856 et seqq.

Lines 65, 66 read first:

> Was she not stepping to my side
>   Upon a silver stair?

In 1856 they became (and remained so through the two trial volumes of 1869):

> Was she not stepping to my side
>   Down all the trembling stair?

This raised a question in Rossetti's mind "whether *trembling* or *tremulous* would be best . . . The first is objectionable because of *stepping* above, but does not the second trip awkwardly?"[3]

The substitution of "towards" for "past" in line 136 and that of "flight" for "lapse" in the next line are certainly for

---

[3] D. G. R. to W. M. R., 27 August 1869 (*L. and M.*, II, 208). W. M. R. replied: "I prefer trembling to tremulous—and think the objection, as connected with 'stepping,' infinitessimal. It would be another matter if the two words occupied like *positions* in the verse" (*Rossetti Papers*, p. 466).

THE BLESSED DAMOZEL

the better, though the second was not made without serious debate.[4] The reading of line 141 in 1856 only:

> And then she laid her arms along
>   The golden barriers

might be preferred on the ground that "cast her arms" implies a movement of rather too much impatience or despair for one of the "blessed." But "golden" in line 142 is an improvement over the "shining" of 1847 because it reminds us happily of "the gold bar" (in 1847 "the silver bar") in line 2 and thus helps to unify the whole poem.

A few passages seem to have given Rossetti special trouble. Lines 3-4 progressed through several states:

Her eyes knew more of rest and shade Than a deep water, even;	1847
Her blue grave eyes were deeper much Than a deep water, even;	1850
Her eyes knew more of rest and shade Than waters stilled at even;	1856
Her eyes were deeper than the depth Of waters stilled at even;	

As usual the 1850 reading is the poorest, largely because of the feebleness of "much"; and it is very instructive to watch the gradual approach to perfect felicity—particularly the change from "even" the adverb to "even" the substantive.

Equally difficult was the opening of stanza viii:

And still she bowed herself and stooped Into the vast waste calm,	1847, 1850
And still she bow'd above the vast Waste seas of worlds that swarm;	1856-1869[2]
And still she bowed herself and stooped Out of the circling charm;	1870[a] et seqq.

[4] *L. and M.*, II, 208, and *Rossetti Papers*, p. 466. W. M. R. liked the "visual impression" of "lapse"; "it looks like sailing through the air without any *motion* of the wings (as one often sees birds), and gives more the idea of serial succession."

In the first version the rime was bad; in the second were too many sibilants, and "swarm" was too obviously rime-forced; in the third there is more meaning—her eagerness, as in line 1, to reach down from heaven to her lover on earth—though "circling charm" is somewhat precious and Marinistic. Similarly we may wonder if Rossetti was finally satisfied with line 123:

THE BLESSED DAMOZEL

Kneel, the unnumbered ransomed heads	1847
Kneel—the unnumber'd solemn heads	1850
Kneel, the unnumber'd ransom'd heads	1856
Kneel, the clear-ranged unnumbered heads	1869[a] et seqq.

But most troublesome of all were lines 37-40:

Heard hardly, some of her new friends,
    Playing at holy games,
Spake gentle-mouthed among themselves
    Their virginal chaste names;   1847, 1850

She scarcely heard her sweet new friends:
    Playing at holy games
Softly they spake among themselves
    Their virginal chaste names;   1856

She scarcely heard her sweet new friends:
    Amid their loving games
Softly they spake among themselves
    Their virginal chaste names;   1869[1]

Heard hardly, some of her new friends,
    Amid their loving games
Spake evermore among themselves
    Their virginal chaste names;   1869[2]-1870[5]

Heard hardly, some of her new friends
    In joy no sorrow claims
Spake evermore among themselves
    Their rapturous new names;   1872, 1873

Around her, lovers newly met
    'Mid deathless love's acclaims,
Spoke evermore among themselves
    Their heart-remembered names;   1881

[xxv]

THE BLESSED DAMOZEL

The first five are evidently inferior, since she might be expected scarcely to hear them if they spoke softly; whereas it was her absorption in her own thoughts which prevented her hearing them; and both "hardly" and "scarcely" are awkward words in poetry. Interesting is the return in 1869² to the first version, except for "loving" instead of "holy" games. The revision of 1872, 1873 discards the "games," but substitutes a line which is weak and too obviously rime-ridden; and in the fourth line introduces a new idea in the "rapturous new names," which points to the contrast between *their* perfect joy and the Damozel's longing for her lover. Finally—and this is the only alteration made in the text of 1881—a fresh substitute is found for the second line and the friends are shown to be likewise filled with longing for their earthly life. But perhaps it is still not entirely satisfying: "Love's acclaims" is affected, we cannot escape the feeling that the rime is to blame; and strictly considered the friends would be *behind* rather than "Around her."⁵

Some of these comments may appear otiose or niggling. My defense would be that in a poem of such delicate workmanship, such remote, rare, and fragile beauty, where so many efforts have been made to get precisely the right word and the right effect, and every choice was difficult,—in a creation so nicely poised between heaven and earth, born in the imagination of a youth of eighteen, cherished and labored over for more than thirty years, while it gathered an accretion of autobiographic meaning—each detail so carefully selected and contributing so much to the whole,—in such a work literally everything deserves to be scrutinized by the reader as it was by the poet.

⁵ I do not understand Dr. Knickerbocker's remark, approving the final version, that "virginal chaste names" or "rapturous new names" are of no interest to the Damozel now, but "heart-remembered names" are. For whether we are expressly told or not, we may be sure she was not listening to them. The point of this last alteration is to show that *all* damozels in heaven are, like the Blessed Damozel, inclined to think of their past existence on earth.

IV

The metrical pattern is alternating 4- and 3-beat lines riming abcbdb. It was not an invention of Rossetti's, having been used by Wordsworth and by Hood (of course with a different music).[1] Apparently it is an extension of the ballad stanza, such as Rossetti would have found in 'The Ancient Mariner' and certainly saw in *Festus*. Where Rossetti actually got it is another question. Mr. Mégroz thought that he got it from Ciullo d'Alcamo's 'Dialogue between a Lover and His Lady,' translated by Rossetti,[2] which goes $a^4b^3c^4b^3d^4b^3ee^5$, by omitting the final couplet. "In this dialogue it is clear that he found the metre and rhythm for 'The Blessed Damozel'," says Mr. Mégroz.[3] Mr. Waller[4] "disposes of" this view by quoting the first stanza of Ciullo and asking, "Who can hear anything of Rossetti's stanza in this?" The answer is obvious. But if one takes the first six lines of the twenty-third stanza, in Rossetti's translation, the case is somewhat different.

> Thou sayest truly, saying that
> I have not any friend:
> A landless stranger, lady mine,
> None but his sword defend.
> One year ago, my love began,
> And now, is this the end?

This is to be sure an exceptional stanza rhythmically, for most of the thirty-two stanzas of the translation are stiffer and cruder and are quite lacking in the freedom, variety, or smoothness of 'The Blessed Damozel.' We may say therefore that the metrical pattern of 'The Blessed Damozel' may have come from

---

[1] Wordsworth in 'The Primrose of the Rock'; Hood in 'The Volunteer' and 'The Dream of Eugene Aram.' Cf. Schipper, *Englische Metrik*, II, 2, pp. 647 f. It has also been used twice by Longfellow, once by Mrs. Browning, and in two other poems by Rossetti.
[2] *The Works*, 1911, pp. 421-427.
[3] *Op. cit.*, p. 167.
[4] In the article cited below, p. xxxi, note 4.

THE BLESSED DAMOZEL

Ciullo—"the metre," but not so confidently "the rhythm"; or it may have come from 'The Ancient Mariner' or from *Festus*; or it may have been re-invented by Rossetti. The question is of no great importance. What *is* important is to observe that at about the same time Rossetti could handle the same metre so differently: so imperfectly, as in his eleventh stanza of Ciullo—

> If thou unto the cloister fly,
>   Thou cruel lady and cold,
> Unto the cloister I will come
>   And by the cloister hold;
> For such a conquest liketh me
>   Much better than much gold; . . .

and so consummately, as in the last stanza of 'The Blessed Damsel' (1847)—

> (I saw her smile.) But soon their flight
>   Was vague in distant spheres.
> And then she laid her arms along
>   The shining barriers,
> And laid her face between her hands,
>   And wept. (I heard her tears.)

The music of a stanza is never to be completely dissociated from its matter. The metrical pattern remains; the tune changes. This is of course a commonplace, but needs repeating, lest we should expect to find the same rhythm in the translation of a twelfth-century Italian poem and in an original poem of the nineteenth. Indeed the very same metre was used with an entirely different effect by Rossetti only two years later, in 'The Card-Dealer'—

> Her fingers let them softly through,
>   Smooth polished silent things;
> And each one as it falls reflects
>   In swift light-shadowings,
> Blood-red and purple, green and blue,
>   The great eyes of her rings.

Still different is Wilde's use of the same stanza in 'The Ballad of Reading Goal,' where, especially with the introduction of internal rime in the first, third, or fifth line, the ballad origin and the influence of Coleridge are more apparent than in Rossetti. There can be no doubt that the languorous effect of prolonging the quatrain is more suitable to 'The Blessed Damozel' than to either of these other poems.

Mr. Mégroz notes "the straightforward rhythm" of stanza xiii, which (he says) "is gradually varied with more complicated effects" as in stanzas vi, ix, x. This is a little puzzling, since the variation would seem to be retrogressive, from stanza xiii to stanza vi.[5] In point of fact the rhythmical movement is varied throughout. The first three stanzas are comparatively regular and the fourth comparatively complicated rhythmically; the fifth, sixth, and seventh alternately regular and complex; and so on. In the last three stanzas the movement is astonishingly varied, whereas in the three immediately preceding it is fairly simple. That is, in the larger rhythm of the whole poem there is constant variety, as there is in the line and stanza rhythm, the norm recurring sufficiently often to make itself felt as a base or point of departure. Which is only to say that the metre is handled with extraordinary skill. This is no doubt more apparent in the final version than in the first, but it is none the less striking in the first version, or even in the second, where an occasional crudity or roughness, as in

[5] He misquotes the fifth line of st. xiii, making it more straightforward than Rossetti did:
> We will step downward to a stream;

and he is of course unconcerned with the variations which Rossetti introduced progressively:
> We will step down as to a stream.
> And we will step down as to a stream.
> We will step down as to a stream.
> As unto a stream we will step down.

THE BLESSED DAMOZEL

> And her hair lying down her back.
>
> And still she bowed herself and stooped
>   Into the vast waste calm,
> Till her bosom's pressure must have made
>   The bar she leaned on warm.

(to say nothing of those stanzas of 1850 which were immediately rejected) has the effect of spontaneity and freshness. The metrical subtlety of the third last stanza, even in the 1847 text, is quite astonishing—

> There will I ask of Christ the Lord
>   Thus much for him and me:—
> Only to live as once on earth
>   At peace,—only to be
> As then awhile, for ever now
>   Together, I and he.

And while a study of the variants is instructive as revealing increased mastery, it is noteworthy that some of the most interesting stanzas metrically (e.g., iv, xvi, xxiii, xxiv) are very little changed in the last text from what they were in the earliest.

v

At the very end of his life, when he was broken in spirit and in health, Rossetti was taken by Hall Caine to Cumberland with the hope of bringing him some comfort and alleviation. On one of the long evenings of this distressful time Rossetti remarked to his companion, after reciting 'Ulalume' and 'The Raven,' "That out of his love for ['The Raven'] while still a boy his own *Blessed Damozel* originated. 'I saw,' he said, 'that Poe had done the utmost it was possible to do with the grief of the lover on earth, and so I determined to reverse the conditions, and give utterance to the yearning of the loved one in heaven.'"[1] This statement is repeated by W. M. R. in the

---

[1] Hall Caine, *Recollections of Dante Gabriel Rossetti*, 1882, p. 284.

Memoir;[2] it is omitted by Hall Caine in the later edition of his *Recollections*;[3] but it has been frequently quoted. How much weight should be allowed to this explanation of the origin of 'The Blessed Damozel,' considering the circumstances under which it was given, it is difficult to know. Most readers will agree that without this hint from Rossetti the association of the two poems would scarcely have been made. They have nothing in common except this 'reversal of the conditions': the lover on earth lamenting the death of his sainted maiden, and the blessed damsel in heaven lamenting her separation from her lover. On the other hand, while it may seem strange that Rossetti had never mentioned the fact before, it is hard to suppose that he would invent the notion ex post facto, even though his mind was far from normal at the time; and we may therefore accept it literally as the originating idea, developed very differently from Poe's treatment because the conditions were really reversed and because Rossetti was so familiar with the "Gothic manner" of Italian mediæval poetry.

The chief proponent of the Italian inspiration of 'The Blessed Damozel' is Professor A. D. Waller.[4] "The general situation of the poem," he says, "obviously reflects the separa-

THE BLESSED DAMOZEL

---

[2] *L. and M.*, I, 107.

[3] London, 1928. Here he says only that Rossetti would at this time repeatedly recite Poe's 'Ulalume' and 'The Raven' (p. 186).

[4] In *Modern Language Review*, XXVI (1931), 129-141. This article was summed up by Professor Waller in his *The Rossetti Family, 1824-1854*, Manchester, 1932, pp. 202 f.: After using Poe as a "preliminary impetus," "he forgot Poe in the thought of Heaven, as depicted in the *Apocalypse* and Dante's *Paradise*, and even in Shelley's *Queen Mab*. The theme is the theme of the *Vita Nuova*, love separated here but to be renewed hereafter. The Damozel, like Beatrice, has 'gone up into high heaven'; her lover sees her in a vision after ten years. Associations from Dante, from the poets of his circle, and even from Petrarch, crowded into the poet's mind as he contemplated the theme, and his stanzas are full of obvious reminiscence, sometimes clearer in the earliest version of the poem than in the later ones.

"The total result is of course not in the least Dantesque.... What he took from Dante and the *Apocalypse* have [sic] been subtly assimilated to the dream of young and ideal love, spiritual in feeling and symbol but only so because still virginal."

THE BLESSED DAMOZEL

tion of Dante and Beatrice. Its theme is the theme of the *Vita Nuova*—'Ita n'è Beatrice in l'alto cielo'." He thinks that "It is surely more than coincidence that the lover has been waiting ten years on earth, before seeing this vision, exactly the length of time which elapses before Dante sees Beatrice in Purgatory"; and he notes the idealization of love and of the lady in both and "the corresponding self-abasement of the lover." It is difficult to take these statements seriously; but perhaps Professor Waller has been unconsciously misled by Kurt Horn's astonishing remark that "Rossettis Blessed Damozel heisst Beatrice."[5] Beyond the mere fact that in both works the lady is in heaven and her lover on earth there is no significant resemblance. The relations between Dante and Beatrice and between the Damozel and her lover are worlds apart; *ten* years is merely a round number; and humility in the lover is everywhere conventional in the poetry of chivalric love. The case is a little different when Professor Waller points out that in a canzone written to Dante 'On the Death of Beatrice' Cino da Pistoia says that Dante

> L'alma vostra che ancora ispera
> Vederla in cielo star nelle sue braccia.
>
> In Heaven still hopes to see her and to be
> Within her arms.[6]

and that Jacopo da Lentino says in a sonnet that he would not care to go to heaven without his lady.[7] The ideas are not strange, but the one gives us corporeal images in heaven and the other suggests the damozel's unhappiness there without her lover. It is likely enough (Professor Waller's "there can be no doubt at all" seems to me too strong) "that the idea of the

---

[5] *Zur Entstehungsgeschichte von Dante Gabriel Rossetti's Dichtungen*, Bernau, 1909, p. 18.
[6] Rossetti's translation, *The Works*, 1911, p. 381.
[7] Cf. Rossetti's translation, *The Works*, 1911, p. 440.

lost damozel waiting in heaven for her lover, and longing for him with a good deal of earthly tenderness, had remained in his mind from the reading of the early Italian poets." Further Professor Waller finds in the cancelled stanza (via) of 1850—

> But in those tracts, with her, it was
>   The peace of utter light
> And silence. For no breeze may stir
>   Along the steady flight
> Of seraphim; no echo there,
>   Beyond all depth or height.

"a reflection of that ultimate peace" of Dante's Tenth Heaven. But while the parallel may be admitted for what it is worth, Rossetti's rejection of his stanza is a witness of a real difference between the spirit of the two poets.

The parallel passages which Professor Waller adduces are these:

>   as low as where this earth
> Spins like a fretful midge.   (ll. 35 ff.)

> Col viso ritornai per tutte e quante
> le sette spere, e vidi questo globo
> tal, ch' io sorrisi del suo vil sembiante.
>   (*Par.* xxii, 133 ff.)

> And the souls mounting up to God
>   Went by her like thin flames.   (ll. 41 f.)

"The spirits in the Seventh Heaven pass up and down the ladder of contemplation as lights, and as a light the soul of Cacciaguida detaches itself from the great cross in the Heaven of Mars, and swoops down to address his descendant."[8]

>   But shall God lift
> The soul whose likeness with thy soul
> Was but its love for thee?   (ll. 99 ff:; first in 1856)

[8] And he adds: "Perhaps it is not fantastic *also* [the italics are mine] to connect the Damozel's 'deep wells of light' with that river of light after drinking from which Dante is made fit for his final ecstatic vision of the Divine Essence"; see *Par.* xxx, 49-51, 61-64.

THE BLESSED DAMOZEL

THE BLESSED DAMOZEL

> Alas, and though the end were reached? ...
>   Was *thy* part understood
> Or borne in trust?   And for her sake
> Shall this too be found good?   (st. xvii*b*, in 1850 only)

Cf. "the spirit of humility that pervades the poetry of the *dolce stil nuovo*," especially in a ballata probably by Cino but ascribed by Rossetti to Dante.[9]

> "We two," she said, "will seek the groves
>   Where the lady Mary is,   (ll. 103 f.)

> La gentil donna che per suo valore
> fu posta da l' altissimo signore
> nel ciel de l' umiltate ov' è Maria.   (*Vita Nuova*, son. xviii)

>   The light thrilled towards her, fill'd
> With angels in strong level flight.   (ll. 136 f.)

Cf. Cavalcanti's sonnet, where his lady "fa tremar di claritate l' a're."[10]

> And then she cast her arms along
>   The golden barriers,
> And laid her face between her hands,
>   And wept. (I heard her tears.)

>   Ella sì lontana
> Come parea, sorrise e riguardommi.   (*Par.* xxxi, 91 f.)[11]

Professor Waller's final comment is modest and even reasonable, but it has the effect of seriously weakening his argument: "Without taking any one of such parallels too seriously, it is impossible to suppose they were without effect in the moulding of Rossetti's poem." His parallels, both of idea and of phrasing, are those of one diligently seeking for parallels. On the

---

[9] Cf. *The Works*, 1911, p. 349.
[10] Cf. Rossetti's translation, *The Works*, 1911, p. 358.
[11] Perhaps the parallel is more significant than Professor Waller's quotations might suggest. His comment is: "She too looked down and smiled, but it was only for a moment—*poi si tornò all' eterna fontana.*" And this seems to me rather to point a difference than a likeness.

other hand, it is hardly to be supposed that a mind saturated as Rossetti's was with Dante and the poets of his circle when he first wrote 'The Blessed Damozel' should not reflect something of their spirit and their language. But the very difficulty of finding precise evidences of relationship is not so much testimony of the absence of relationship as of the thoroughness with which Rossetti wrought his own poem from his own imagination rather than piecing it together with shapes and colors from his reading.

In a similar way traces of Coleridge and Keats and Shelley and even Goethe have been found in 'The Blessed Damozel.' The curious may like to see them in the articles already cited. But as it requires a special *flair* to detect sources and influences of this sort, so it requires a special ability to see any profit in them. A poet writes what he knows and what he imagines. What his imagination bodies forth is dependent upon what he knows. Some poets, like Milton—"the celestial thief"—borrow freely but recast the borrowing in their own mould. There is a peculiar exhilaration (for some) in tracking phrases and ideas to their source, and there may be a real service in this when the concern is not merely to point the parallel but rather to observe how and why a poet has reworked the old material. The question is not: Where did he get it? but What did he do with it? With Rossetti, however, hardly any of the forms of Quellenforschung can have any interest; for he was always careful, and even anxious, to avoid the appearance of borrowing. It was not a matter, with him, of concealing his indebtedness so much as of justifying his own originality. Though he was familiar with many poets, his best work was never derivative. Though his range was limited, he never sought to enlarge his experience from the poetry of others. He preferred to develop his own vein. It is for this reason that we can gain more in the study of his

THE BLESSED DAMOZEL poetry by learning about him as he lived and moved among his friends than by comparing him with his predecessors. He was essentially an autobiographic writer. His experience was narrow, but it was his own, and from it he wrought his poetry.

Only in his earliest verse do we hear echoes of his reading, and even then but rarely, as in 'A Last Confession.' Generally the parallels are accidental and without significance, as in the opening lines of 'Rose Mary':

> Mary mine that art Mary's Rose,
> Come in to me from the garden-close,

and Tennyson's

> Come into the garden, Maud;

or the result of deliberate imitation, as in the ballads. The extraordinary degree to which 'The Blessed Damozel' resists our efforts to detect reminiscences of that Italian poetry with which his mind must have been saturated is proof of his peculiar originality and independence. Without Dante and his fellow poets 'The Blessed Damozel' would not have been what it is, could hardly have been written at all; yet the influence of Dante is vague and general, prevasive rather than precise.

A certain light is thrown on this problem by a letter of Leigh Hunt's and Rossetti's comment thereon.[12] Early in 1848 Rossetti sent Hunt some translations and original poems, including 'The Blessed Damozel,' and Hunt replied (31 March), finding fault with the versification of the translations: "I guess indeed that you are altogether not so musical as pictorial. But, when I came to the originals of your own, I recognized an unquestionable poet, thoughtful, imaginative, and with rare powers of expression. I hailed you at once as such, without any misgiving; and, besides your Dantesque heavens (without any hell to spoil them), admired the complete and genial round

---

[12] *L. and M.*, I, 122 f.; II, 38.

of your sympathies with humanity." This last may be somewhat surprising; but it would seem that Rossetti was a little disturbed by the phrase "Dantesque heavens," for he wrote soon after to his Aunt Charlotte Polidori:

> Where Hunt, in his kind letter, speaks of my "Dantesque heavens," he refers to one or two of the poems the scene of which is laid in the celestial regions, and which are written in a kind of Gothic manner which I suppose he is pleased to think belongs to the school of Dante.

"One or two poems" I do not understand unless it refers merely to 'The Blessed Damozel'; no other early poem is known which has a scene in the celestial regions, though Rossetti may have had 'Ave' in mind. It does not help us much to know that Rossetti thought of his poem as written "in a kind of Gothic manner," but it certainly appears that he deprecated the association of 'The Blessed Damozel' with the school of Dante. Since this runs directly counter to the conclusion we have just reached, it seems necessary to assume that Rossetti was unaware of the effect of his study of the Italian poets. (Mr. Mégroz' view that Rossetti was disingenuous in writing so to his aunt may be dismissed as without reasonable foundation.) And perhaps after all, this is the best account of the matter: though permeated with the poetry of Dante and the *dolce stil nuova* Rossetti was unconscious of writing in their manner when he composed 'The Blessed Damozel.' A "kind of Gothic" it might be, since it was mediæval or at least not modern; but "Dantesque" he would not admit. Nor is it at all Dantesque in the sense of imitating Dante or of representing his tone or spirit.[13]

Among the contributory influences the *Apocalypse* has been frequently mentioned (for example, by Mr. Waller); the full-

---

[13] Dr. Knickerbocker almost wholly rejects the ideas of Waller. The heaven of 'The Blessed Damozel', he says, "is Dantesque in only one stanza [*via*] and that stanza was eliminated in the second published version of the poem."

THE BLESSED DAMOZEL

est account being Lafcadio Hearn's.[14] He notes that all the angels in *Revelation* are clothed in white, as the Damozel's lover will be (l. 74: and we recall that in the 1847 text she herself was white-robed, l. 9). "The deep wells of light" (l. 76) wherein as in a stream the lovers will bathe "in God's sight" suggest the "pure river of water of life, clear as crystal, proceeding out of the throne of God" (*Rev.* xxii, 1). The lamps beside "that shrine" (ll. 79-81) may be reminiscent of the "seven lamps of fire burning before the throne" *(Rev.* iv, 5). The image of prayers "each like a little cloud" (ll. 83-84) is more remotely suggestive of the "odours, which are the prayers of saints" (*Rev.* v, 8) and of the incense which was to be offered "with the prayers of all saints upon the golden altar which was before the throne" (*Rev.* viii, 3). "That living mystic tree" (l. 86) is perhaps the tree of life in the final version (*Rev.* xxii, 2). All these parallels, it should be observed, moreover, occur in the space of a dozen lines.[15]

To these similarities may be added the seven stars in the right hand of the figure in *Rev.* i, 16 and the woman with a crown of twelve stars upon her head *(Rev.* xii, 1), which together may have helped to produce Rossetti's sixth line. But what is perhaps more interesting and important is that in the *Apocalypse* itself Rossetti could have found that same combination of definite visual imagery and non-visual symbolic metaphor for which 'The Blessed Damozel' is famous. Just as we have "the gold bar of heaven," "Her hair . . . Was yellow like

[14] 'The Blessed Damozel' was a difficult poem to set before Japanese students, and Hearn did simply what he could; cf. his attempt, *Pre-Raphaelite and Other Poets*, New York, 1922, pp. 20-35.

[15] The further Biblical echo in l. 54 and *Job* xxxviii, 7 ("when the morning stars sang together") has been frequently noted. Hearn drew attention also to the probable source of the idea in l. 71, viz. *Matthew* xviii, 19: "if two of you shall agree on earth as touching anything that they shall ask, it shall be done for them." None of these parallels is noted by F. Holthausen, "D. G. Rossetti und die Bibel," in *Germanisch-romanische Monatsschrift*, XIII (1925), 310-312; XIV (1926), 73-76.

ripe corn," and "her bosom must have made The bar she leaned on warm" beside "she saw Time like a pulse shake fierce Through all the worlds," "the light thrilled towards her, fill'd With angels," and "I heard her tears"; so we have in the *Apocalypse* "And the first beast was like a lion, and the second beast like a calf, and the third beast had a face as a man, and the fourth beast was like a flying eagle. And the four beasts had each of them six wings about him" (*Rev.* iv, 7 f.) and "they need no candle, neither the light of the sun" *(Rev.* xxii, 5), which are literal and precise, beside such abstract images as "he that sat on the cloud thrust in his sickle on the earth; and the earth was reaped" (*Rev.* xiv, 16), "a sea of glass mingled with fire" *(Rev.* xv, 2), and the four angels "holding the four winds of the earth" (*Rev.* vii, 1). It is not so much that Rossetti may have remembered and used certain tropes from the *Apocalypse;* or that both kinds of imagery, the visual and the non-visual (like Shakespeare's "sea of troubles" or Milton's "Care sat on his faded cheek"), are not common elsewhere; but that in a familiar work describing extra-terrestrial phenomena he must have noted a mingling of simple, directly descriptive imagery with the indirect, suggestive, or symbolic use of natural details. I am not in the least concerned to insist on the *Apocalypse* as a source, or even a model of which he made conscious use, but rather to suggest that the poet's active mind would readily observe such a complex method, perhaps without analyzing it too clearly, and when the similar problem of making imaginary scenes vivid was presented to him he would instinctively adopt a similar technique.

More than fifteen years ago Professor McKillop suggested that the 'sources' of 'The Blessed Damozel' were to be found in Philip James Bailey's *Festus*.[16]

[16] Alan D. McKillop, *"Festus* and *The Blessed Damozel,"* in *Modern Language Notes,* XXXIV (1919), 93-97. This article was apparently overlooked

THE BLESSED DAMOZEL

> In this mysterious, allegorical,
> Mythical, theological, odd story,

there is so much that one would hardly be surprised to find 'The Blessed Damozel' there with all the rest. No one reads it now, although it contains not a little that is worth reading still, but eighty or ninety years ago it was extremely popular. It is almost a miracle of volubility; its style and spirit are in most ways poles distant from the style and spirit of Rossetti's poem; yet we know that Rossetti read *Festus* "over and over again for a while" just at the time when he was composing 'The Blessed Damozel.'[17] And granting the prior claims of Poe's 'Raven' as the inciting incident, granting also all that may properly be urged for the general influence of Dante and the early Italian poets, the similarities between it and *Festus* are interesting enough to warrant our attention. In the first place, the general situation of love between a mortal and a lady in heaven, familiar of course in Dante, appears here also.

> I have a love on earth, and one in Heaven,

says Festus to Lucifer in their first conversation; and Lucifer tells him—

> I am not in love;
> But I have ofttimes heard mine angels call
> Most piteously on their lost loves in Heaven.[18]

In "Another and a Better World" Festus meets Angela, the first and apparently the purest of his loves, whose death had set him in Lucifer's path.

> ANGELA. I am a spirit, Festus; and I love
> Thy spirit, and shall love, when once like mine,
> More than we ever did or can even now.

---

by Mr. Waller and Mr. Knickerbocker. I have incorporated in what follows a good part of Professor McKillop's article and added something of my own. His citations are from the first American edition, Boston, 1845; mine are from the "Third Edition, with Additions," London, 1848.

[17] *L. and M.*, I, 89.   [18] *Festus*, p. 5, col. 2.

>   Pure spirits are of Heaven all heavenly.
>   Yet marvel not to meet me in this guise. . . .
>   We wander in what way we will through all
>   Or any of these worlds, and whereso'er
>   We are, there Heaven is, here, and there too, God.
>   FESTUS. Thou dost remember me?
>   ANGELA.   Ay and every thought
>   And look of love which thou hast lent to me,
>   Comes daily through my memory as stars
>   Wear through the dark.
>   FESTUS.   And art thou happy, love?
>   ANGELA. Yes: I am happy when I can do good. . . .
>   . . . They who have come
>   From earth, or other orb, use the same powers,
>   Passions, and purposes, they had ere death. . . .
>   My love, we shall be happy here.
>   FESTUS.   Shall I
>   Ever come here?
>   ANGELA.   Thou mayst. I will pray for thee,
>   And watch thee.
>   FESTUS. Thou wilt have, then, need to weep.
>   This heart must run its orbit. Pardon thou
>   Its many sad deflections. It will return
>   To thee and to the primal goal of Heaven. . . .
>   . . . If aught can make me seek
>   Other to be than that lost soul I fear me,
>   It is that thou lovest me. . . .
>   ANGELA. The rainbow dies in Heaven, and not on earth;
>   But love can never die; from world to world,
>   Up the high wheel of Heaven, it lives for aye.
>   Remember that I wait thee, hoping, here.
>   Life is the brief disunion of that nature
>   Which hath been one and same in Heaven ere now,
>   And shall be yet again, renewed by death.
>   Come to me when thou diest!
>   FESTUS.   I will, I will.
>   ANGELA.   Then, in each other's arms, we will waft through
>   space,
>   Spirit in spirit, one! or we will dwell
>   Among these immortal groves; or watch new worlds,
>   As, like the great thoughts of a Maker-mind,
>   They are rounded out of chaos. . . .

THE BLESSED DAMOZEL

THE BLESSED DAMOZEL

> That thou right soon mayst fold unto thy heart
> The blissful consciousness of separate
> Oneness with God, in Him in whom alone
> The saved are deathless, shall become, for thee,
> My earliest, earnest, and most constant prayer.[19]

In a much later scene, though the physical setting is different, the emotional situation is partially parallel. Elissa, another love of Festus, is dying, and longs to see him again.

> Oh! he will come!
> He must know how I love him. It is long —
> Long since I saw him: I am ill with waiting.
> And I will fancy him coming to me now—
> Now he is thinking of me, loving me—
> He sees me—flies to me, half out of breath—
> His hand is on my arm—he looks on me—
> And puts my long locks backwards—God! Thy ban
> Lies upon waking dreams.[20]

The remainder of this scene, in which Lucifer confesses to Elissa that he also has loved her, is the most (perhaps the only) moving passage in the whole work; it is certainly the kind which remains in a reader's memory.

A great deal of the imagery of *Festus* is vague and magniloquent; the concreteness and simplicity of detail characteristic of 'The Blessed Damozel' is not Bailey's staple; yet his conception of heaven is often as earthly as Rossetti's—

> ... for God
> Makes to each spirit its peculiar Heaven;—
> And yet is Heaven a bright reality,
> As this or any of yon worlds.[21]

> But thinkest thou the future is a state
> More positive than this; or that it can be
> Aught but another present, full of cares,
> And toils, perhaps, and duties;[22]

> ... yon streams where spirits sport
> Quaffing immortal life.[23]

[19] *Festus*, pp. 38-39.
[20] *Festus*, p. 94, col. 1.
[21] *Festus*, p. 9, col. 2.
[22] *Festus*, p. 17, col. 2.
[23] *Festus*, p. 48, col. 1.

Occasionally we are reminded distinctly of some of Rossetti's pictures. Lucifer is conducting Festus through interstellar spaces, and bids him—

THE BLESSED DAMOZEL

> Look downwards from this coping of the world;
> And know that down to the profoundest depth
> Of utter space, where not an atom mars
> The void invisible, it were easier far
> To cast a line and calculate its rate,
> Or pierce all space, nor cross the path of light,
> Than fathom man's dark heart or sound his soul.[24]

Finally, here are a few fragments of possible significance:

> The sun's light
> Floweth and ebbeth daily like the tides.[25]

> Seven thousand years of years.[26]

> until at last
> Earth took her shining station as a star,
> In heaven's dark hall, high up the crowd of worlds.[27]

> And loving as we two have loved
> In spirit and in heart,
> Whether to space or star removed,
> God will not bid us part.[28]

> Earth fluttered like a dead leaf in the blast.[29]

> she spake as with the voice
> Of spheral harmony.[30]

> Oh! when the thoughts of other joyous days— . . .
> Are falling gently on the memory
> Like autumn's leaves.[31]

> A spirit came and gave me wings of light.[32]

> High o'er all height, God sat upon His throne.
> Downwards He bent: and, as a grain of sand,
> He lifted up our globe. Then from His hand,
> As 'twere in pity, bowled the ingrate sphere,

[24] *Festus*, p. 47, col. 2.
[25] *Festus*, p. 11, col. 1.
[26] *Festus*, p. 26, col. 2.
[27] *Festus*, p. 31, col. 2.
[28] *Festus*, p. 45, col. 1.
[29] McKillop, *op. cit.*, p. 333.
[30] *Festus*, p. 71, col. 1.
[31] *Festus*, p. 81, col. 1.
[32] *Festus*, p. 85, col. 1.

THE BLESSED DAMOZEL

> Which rushed like ruin down its dark career.
> And high the air's blue billows rolled and swelled
> On many an island world mine eye beheld.[33]

> till God's son
> Laid o'er the black abyss a bridge of light.[34]

Other readers will doubtless find more crumbs of this sort; but these are sufficient for the purpose.

A curious detail which may be felt to establish the relationship of *Festus* and 'The Blessed Damozel' more than any such similarities remains to be mentioned. This is the note of the lover's unworthiness to join his beloved in heaven, which appeared first in the text of 1850 (stanza xvii*b*) and was much softened in statement in the next version. In both texts it goes quite beyond the conventional view of a lover's unworthiness according to the Courtly Love tradition; in the cancelled stanza xvii*b* of 1850 it suggests a religious unfitness utterly unnecessary and inappropriate in the poem, but entirely consonant with the attitude of Festus, who is separated from Angela by his compact with Lucifer. Without *Festus* there is no very plausible explanation of this jarring note in the poem.

It is perhaps worth observing also that four stanzas of the song 'My gypsy man'[35]—the first, third, fourth, and one other, have the same metre as that of 'The Blessed Damozel.'

In these matters of source and influence it is always difficult to be certain and even more difficult to attach a proper value to the phenomena; but inasmuch as Rossetti is known to have read *Festus* enthusiastically—"over and over again"—just before or when his poem was written, we cannot be wrong in believing that, though the parallels will not satisfy all demands, *Festus* was an important contributory influence.[36] If

---

[33] *Festus*, p. 99, col. 2.   [34] *Festus*, p. 105, col. 1.   [35] *Festus*, p. 24.
[36] Professor McKillop's conclusions were: "it is evident that Rossetti's central idea is found highly developed in Bailey, and moreover that both

'The Raven' gave him the single idea of representing the lady's lament in heaven for her still living lover, and Dante gave him indirectly a great deal of the definiteness of sensible imagery, in Pater's phrase, along with the bare similarity of Beatrice in heaven and Dante on earth (which he did not develop with any approach to closeness, for to do so would have been absurdly daring), there still remains a great deal of room for Bailey's influence in stirring his imagination. Perhaps few persons, reading *Festus*—to compare great things with small (in either direction!)—would be reminded of 'The Blessed Damozel' or think of the two poems as similar; they are incommensurable. Nevertheless there may be bonds between them which defy analytical tabulation or the usual methods of parallel-passage hunters. What can be found in *Festus* resembling 'The Blessed Damozel' I have tried to set forth: it is not altogether impressive. But if the process is reversed, if after finishing a perusal of *Festus* one reads through 'The Blessed Damozel' the result is surprising. Parts of the latter poem seem like a distillation of Bailey's dilute imagery and diffuse visions. It would be bold to say that the one is the quintessence of certain portions of the other, but there would be a kind of truth in the statement. Such things are never susceptible of proof, they can only be intuitively apprehended; and I report my impression, leaving the rest to such as may care to repeat my experiment.

It is a strange parentage, Poe, Bailey, and Dante, for 'The Blessed Damozel,' which in no wise derogates from the extraordinary originality of Rossetti. Nothing ever springs from nothing. But the processes of the creative imagination are ob-

THE BLESSED DAMOZEL

poets use on occasion the same kind of cosmic imagery, visualize the interstellar spaces in much the same way . . . it seems clear to probation, I think, that even though *The Raven* gave Rossetti the initial suggestion for the poem, and even though his Italian background gave him a certain amount of detail, his enthusiastic study of *Festus* markedly influenced his formulation of the central idea and the imagery by which he developed it."

THE BLESSED DAMOZEL scure—even so elaborate and brilliant a piece of Quellenforschung as Professor Lowes' study of Coleridge only emphasizes this—and when all is said we are rather to marvel at the resulting miracle than to take any satisfaction from discovering the ingredients.

VI

One way to appreciate 'The Blessed Damozel' is to look at the other poems of Rossetti written at about the same time. The two juvenile prose pieces 'Roderick and Rosalba' and 'Sorrentino' may be left out of account. The two juvenile ballads 'William and Marie' and 'Sir Hugh the Heron' are of more significance as showing Rossetti's precocity at imitation and his early interest in the popular ballads. How many of the old ballads he had read in 1847 we do not know, but apparently he was acquainted with Percy's *Reliques*.[1] Scott's verse narratives were already familiar to him; and it is to Scott that he refers in his comment on 'Sir Hugh.'[2] He would have absorbed also the mediævalism of Keats and Coleridge, to say nothing of pseudo- and semi-mediæval romances and romantic tales in great numbers.[3] In 1847 also he came under the spell of Browning. His own original work of this year includes a first draft of 'Jan Van Hunks,' 'Jenny,' and 'Ave'; the sonnets 'For an Annunciation' and 'Retro me, Sathana'; 'My Sister's Sleep,' 'On Mary's Portrait,' 'To Mary in Summer,' 'Epitaph for Keats,' and the stanzas on Arthur Stanhope (which are in the metre of 'The Blessed Damozel'); and "also the opening portion of *Dante at Verona, A Last Confession*, and *The Bride's Prelude*."[4] Of these thirteen pieces only two need be considered now. The Annunciation sonnet is interesting for

---

[1] *L. and M.*, I, 98.
[2] "When I wrote it [at the age of twelve to fourteen], the only English poet I had read was Sir W. Scott, as is plain enough in it" (*The Works*, 1911, p. 643). Cf. also *L. and M.*, I, 85.
[3] *L. and M.*, I, 81 ff., 100 ff.   [4] *L. and M.*, I, 107.

its 'Catholicism,' and at least the sestet resembles 'The Blessed Damozel' in tone. 'My Sister's Sleep' has an interest for its simplicity and imaginative realism in some ways suggestive of 'The Blessed Damozel.' In 'Jenny' (though the first version is apparently lost, and without knowing how much of the present text is due to later revisions we cannot speak securely of the poem as a work of 1847) there is also much of the promise and achievement of 'The Blessed Damozel,' but in a different strain. Of 'On Mary's Portrait' I have said something elsewhere; it has likewise the simplicity and directness and vividness of description of 'The Blessed Damozel,' and one stanza (the twelfth) is distinctly reminiscent of it in spirit if not in substance.[5]

Mr. Mégroz pointed to the "family likeness" between 'The Blessed Damozel' and 'The Staff and Scrip,'[6] (not written until 1849), and the same likeness exists in 'The Bride's Prelude,' begun "very little later" than 'The Blessed Damozel.'[7] The stanza is again an extension of the ballad stanza, i.e. the first three lines begin the same, $a^4b^3c^4$; then instead of a fourth line, b^3, we have two lines cc^4, producing just the effect of suspense and retarded movement, the close atmosphere and minute description, wanted in the introductory passages. Again we are on uncertain ground without knowing how much of the present form of the poem is due to revision, but me may recognize kinship with the "definiteness of sensible imagery" and the suggestive rather than literal descriptive details so characteristic of 'The Blessed Damozel,' as well as the archaic language.

>Amelotte laughed into the air
> With eyes that sought the sun:
>But where the walls in long brocade
>Were screened, as one who is afraid
>Sat Aloÿse within the shade.

[5] *Dante Gabriel Rossetti, An Analytical List of Manuscripts in the Duke University*, Durham, N. C., 1931, pp. 26 ff., 67 ff.
[6] Mégroz, p. 234; cf. also p. 260.   [7] *L. and M.*, I, 107.

THE BLESSED DAMOZEL

And even in shade was gleam enough
    To shut out full repose
From the bride's 'tiring-chamber, which
Was like the inner altar-niche
Whose dimness worship has made rich.

Within the window's heaped recess
    The light was counterchanged
In blent reflexes manifold
From perfume-caskets of wrought gold
And gems the bride's hair could not hold,

All thrust together: and with these
    A slim-curved lute, which now,
At Amelotte's sudden passing there,
Was swept in somewise unaware,
And shook to music the close air.

Against the haloed lattice-panes
    The bridesmaid sunned her breast;
Then to the glass turned tall and free,
And braced and shifted daintily
Her loin-belt through her côte-hardie.

"Côte-hardie" is own cousin to "cithern and citole"—stunning words deliberately culled in the reading room of the British Museum.

But it is in the first 'Ave' poem that we find the nearest resemblance to the mood and manner of 'The Blessed Damozel.'[8] In the Trial Books of 1869 Rossetti called this poem a hymn "written as a prologue to a series of designs." At one time in 1847 it was "no. 2" of the projected "Songs of the Art Catholic"; and perhaps then 'The Blessed Damozel' was no. 1. The remainder of Rossetti's note in 1869 is somewhat cryptic: "Art still identifies herself with all faith for her own purposes; and the emotional influence here employed demands above all an inner standing-point." But with the help of William Michael Rossetti we gather that already at this time, 1847, the Pre-

---

[8] The first form is printed in *The Works*, 1911, pp. 661 f. It contains 63 lines, as against 112 lines of the later version. Cf. also *Analytical List*, p. 10.

Raphaelite ideas were forming obscurely. Rossetti's standing-point was the mediæval "sentiment" of early Italian art, "Catholic" being used not with reference to the dogma of the Church but to the "conceptions and point of view" of the Church as they appear in pictorial art of the fourteenth and early fifteenth centuries. If this statement is vague, so no doubt also were Rossetti's sentiments, and we must gain what clarity we can from the poems themselves.[9]

In execution the first 'Ave' shows the same uncertainties of language and rhythm which we find in 'On Mary's Portrait,' in great contrast to the sureness of the 1847 text of 'The Blessed Damozel': The fourth line—

> With the shadow of the Heaven-roof

is lame; the fourteenth and twenty-seventh halt badly—

> And the sorrow we have seemth to last.
> Groundstone of the great Mystery.

And so on. Expressions like "that olden once," "greenly jubilant" (of the leaves of the "Threefold Plant"), and "Godshine" are clearly experimental. On the other hand—

> And a mystic quiet in thine eyes
> Born of the hush of Paradise

and

> But the slow comfort loitereth

and

> Sometimes it even seems to us
> That we are overbold when thus
> We cry and hope we shall be heard;—
> Being much less than a short word,—
> Mere shadow that abideth not,—
> Dusty nothing, soon forgot.

---

[9] Hall Caine remarks, on the mingling of the language of religion with Rossetti's love poems: "but this is only another proof that the deepest thing in him was the spirit of the old type of Italian Catholic" (*Recollections*, 1928, p. 54).

THE BLESSED DAMOZEL

show not only some of the mastery, but also some of the style and feeling of 'The Blessed Damozel.' Felicitous phrases and successful rhythms however are within the reach of many a second-rate amateur; it is the uniform and consistent excellence of 'The Blessed Damsel' of 1847 which distinguished it from the other work of this year (so far as we have it in the earliest form) and mark it as an extraordinary achievement for a youth of nineteen.

VII

Critical remarks on 'The Blessed Damozel' have been of course very numerous, if often not very helpful. It is the kind of poem which does not lend itself to commentary in the usual formulas; for it is a highly irrational work, and whatever one says about it by way of appreciation is likely to be inept. But I choose two or three observations for their curious interest.

It is not surprising that Max Nordau should have found a place for Rossetti in his grand catalogue of 'degenerates,' or that he should have classified the Pre-Raphaelites under the heading of Mysticism; but it is astonishing that with egoism, emotionalism, and despondency as his stigmata of degeneracy and with all of Rossetti's poetry before him, he should have concentrated on 'The Blessed Damozel.'[1] To be sure, he does see a point in 'Troy-Town,' but regards the fundamental idea as absurd and the refrains as mere "muttering"; the poem's extreme eroticism he passes without comment. And in 'Eden Bower' he notices only the "absolutely senseless phrases" of the refrains as "a startling example of echolalia." (The rest of Rossetti's poetry reveals to him "the same mixture of transcendentalism and sensuality, the same shadowy ideation, the same senseless combinations of mutually incompatible ideas . . .

---

[1] Max Nordau, *Degeneration*, Translated from the Second Edition, New York, 1895, Book II, ch. ii, pp. 86 ff. If Nordau used only the Tauchnitz edition, he knew only the *Poems* of 1870—those which roused Buchanan.

the brain-work of weak degenerate minds.") But to the analysis of 'The Blessed Damozel' he devotes five large pages to show, he says, Rossetti's "parasitic battening on the body of Dante," as well as "some of the most characteristic peculiarities of the mental working of the mystic's brain." To begin with: "The whole of this description of a lost love, who looks down upon him from a heaven imagined as a palace, with paradisaical decorations, is a reflection of Dante's *Paradiso* (Canto iii.), where the Blessed Virgin speaks to the poet from the moon." The image of "waters still'd at even" comes from

THE BLESSED DAMOZEL

> . . . per acque nitide e tranquille,
> Non sì profonde che i fondi sien persi.
> *Par*. iii, 11-12.

"The 'lilies in her hand' he gets from the Old Masters, yet even here there is a slight ring of the morning greeting from the *Purgatorio* (Canto xxx.), '*Manibus o date lilia plenis*'." This is all we learn about the indebtedness of 'The Blessed Damozel' to Dante, except the pungent distinction that Dante "was a mystic from ignorance, not from the weakmindedness of degeneration," and that while Dante followed the best knowledge of his day, "Rossetti's *Blessed Damozel* is not based upon the scientific knowledge of his time, but upon a mist of undeveloped germs of ideas in constant mutual strife." Rossetti is "incapable of the necessary attention" to take in "the realities of the world" with Dante's "keenly penetrating eyes of an observer." For the rest, Nordau finds the use of the mystical numbers three and seven without significance (though in the preceding paragraph they are "mysterious and holy" and "of deep meaning, which the intuitive reader may try to understand"); the computation of "ten years of years" is "thoroughly mystical. It means, that is, absolutely nothing." The details of the picture

THE BLESSED DAMOZEL of God's house high over the abyss of space cannot be united "into one complete picture." The notion of the two lovers bathing together (he adds the "together") in God's sight moves him to remark: "Mystical reverie never fails to be accompanied by sensuality." And the damozel's tears (in the last line) are incomprehensible to him.

The blessed maiden after her death lives in the highest bliss, in a golden palace, in the presence of God and the Blessed Virgin. What pains her now? That her beloved is not yet with her? Ten years of mortal men are to her as a single day. Even if it be her beloved's destiny to live to be a very old man, she will at most have to wait only five or six of her days until he appears at her side.

—So much for clarity and reason.

The perverseness of these judgments need not concern us. What might properly be called decadent in Rossetti Nordau seems to have missed altogether; his dictum that the Pre-Raphaelites misunderstood Ruskin's misunderstandings might be turned on him. But his comments on "the Anglo-Norman word 'damozel'" and on the five names in lines 107-108 have a value in spite of his intention.

By the word 'girl' we should just think of a girl and nothing else. 'Damozel' awakens in the consciousness of the English reader obscure ideas of slim, noble ladies in the tapestries of old castles, of haughty Norman knights in mail, of something remote, ancient, half forgotten; 'damozel' carries back the contemporary beloved into the mysterious depths of the Middle Ages, and spiritualizes her into the enchanted figure of a ballad. This one word awakens all the crepuscular moods which the body of romantic poets and authors have bequeathed as a residum in the soul of the contemporary reader.

... the five names arouse gliding shadowy ideas of beautiful young maidens, 'Rosalys' those of roses and lilies as well; and the two verses together diffuse a glamour of faerie, as if one were roaming at ease in a garden of flowers, where between lilies and roses slender white and rosy maidens pace to and fro.

Another curious interpretation of 'The Blessed Damozel' is to be found in a pamphlet by A. G.[2] called "A Dream of Fair Women" (London, 1883). This is dedicated to the belief that Rossetti "is entitled to a place among those who are, by reason of spiritual insight and aspiration, empowered to bring effectual succour to their fellow-men." A. G. is concerned both with the poem and with the picture of the same name. "Though in the poem," he says at first, "she is distinguished from Mary, in the picture 'The Blessed Damozel' is manifestly 'Our Lady'." Later, of the poem itself:

THE BLESSED DAMOZEL

'The Blessed Damozel' we understand to be, if we are to penetrate to its deepest and most fundamental meaning, a revelation of the woman-heart of God. She discloses the unforsaking Pitifulness of Divine Love, the eternal and infinite Compassion. Thus is the sacrament of Beauty at length interpreted; it is one with Purity; it is one with Charity. The pure only are passionate; and their yearning desires are creative and redemptive, dowered with something of a divine energy, living flames from Love's central shrine. . . . So the Blessed Damozel is *at home* with God. Sharing His saving purpose, she is both victim and advocate, all-enduring and dauntless. . . . Put this picture and this poem together, and it is difficult in all the rich stores of Catholic art to find so adequate an exposition of the spiritual significance of Mary.

This must have pleased Christina, but she herself read the poem otherwise.

'The Blessed Damozel' does, as Christina said, fall short of "expressing the highest view." In truth, it falls short of expressing any view at all. But it is a wonderfully decorative piece, a "painted paradise" in the style we may now quite securely call Pre-Raphaelite. There had been nothing quite like its "angelic beauty" or its magic before, and no one will care to imitate it. It has something of the slightly stiff simplicity of the early Florentine school, to be sure, and is com-

[2] The Rev. Alfred Gurney, vicar of St. Barnabas, Pimlico, with whom Christina corresponded for several years beginning in 1883.

THE BLESSED DAMOZEL posed in a kind of Gothic manner; but in 1847 Rossetti knew little or nothing of the early Florentines. He had, on the other hand, a poetic instinct which enabled him to *create,* before its formal inauguration in the P. R. B. and its official promulgation in *The Germ,* the nineteenth-century Pre-Raphaelite school of poetry and painting, with its fragile beauty, its accumulation of sensuous detail to express a half-spiritual emotion, its gathering together of quasi-mediæval colors in strange language and of pale earthly realities in human form, its peculiar blending of this world and another world of the poet's fancy. The Paradise of Dante sprang from an austere and devout imagination; the Heaven from which the Blessed Damozel leaned down towards earth, and in which she waited for the coming of her lover is a copy of this world done in pastel tints, a very earthly paradise, adorned with some of the properties of the Roman church. The religion we find there is the religion of chivalric love, neither pagan nor Christian, but that substitute for religion which the Middle Ages invented when Christianity had failed them and it seemed necessary to take refuge in a dream. Without having himself known it before, Rossetti rediscovered it, and for a little while it was so real to him that he could recreate it in two poems, 'The Blessed Damozel' and the first 'Ave,' and in a stanza of the first 'Portrait.' It was a dream-world of the innocent idealization of love. Then came Elizabeth Siddal, and then Jenny, whose later name was Fanny, and love had a different meaning for him. He found refuge elsewhere than with the Lady Mary and aureoled angels singing

> To their citherns and citoles.

It is easy to idealize what we have but imperfectly realized; but blood will not flow in angelic veins. After 1851 Rossetti as artist could well enough recover the mood and attitude of

1847 to improve many of the details of the poem; after 1851 he could not have conceived 'The Blessed Damozel' at all. A few years later, when a new Beatrice had appeared to him, and he had become acquainted with love in many forms, he could write the tortured sonnets of 'The House of Life' (where there are only faint and formal copies of the Dantesque heavens) and express the complicated emotions of 'The Stream's Secret'; but he had left for ever the circling charm of that youthful dream-paradise for the mature pleasures of 'Troy Town' and 'Eden Bower.'

It is not fanciful (I think) to see even in the sensuous unrealities of this early poem already a hint of that duality which runs through all of his life and his poetry. The conflict of southern blood and northern background was too strong for his power of will; for in that conflict he sought an easy escape, and spirit succumbed to body. In 'The Blessed Damozel' however the struggle has not yet come—there was a different fusion because love was then only a painted image, as remote from experience as the gold bar of heaven. The elements of opposition are there nevertheless, though in solution still. The damozel is very human both in her unhappiness among the angels and in her eagerness for reunion with her lover; her bosom is warm indeed. We might not care to come upon the two lovers lying.

> i' the shadow of
> That living mystic tree

which is frequented by the Holy Ghost. We are not convinced that "the dear Mother" of God will approve either the damozel's pride or her passion. We wonder if it is quite enough for her to pray Christ in heaven

> Only to live as once on earth
> With Love,—only to be,
> As then a while, for ever now
> Together, I and he.

THE BLESSED DAMOZEL   But these scruples of evangelical respectability are altogether absurd in a fictitious heaven; they are altogether irrelevant.[a] Yet we may be permitted to discern in this easy intermingling of sacred and profane the seeds of a tendency which would produce bitter fruit if allowed to develop at all. And in this way 'The Blessed Damozel' foreshadows the Love and Change and Fate of 'The House of Life.'

[a] It is amusing to recall that this is the only poem in the 1870 volume to which Buchanan would allow a qualified praise: "In spite of its affected title, and of numberless affectations throughout the text, the 'Blessed Damozel' has merits of its own, and a few lines of real genius."

The Blessed Damozel

THE TEXTS

On the following pages are printed, first, the text of the Morgan manuscript; second, the text from *The Germ*, No. 2, February 1850, pp. 80-83; third, the text from *The Oxford and Cambridge Magazine*, 1856, pp. 713-715; and, fourth, the final text of *Poems*, 1881, with a collation of all the variants. In the first three versions the stanzas are numbered according to their position in the final text.

The sigla, for the collation, are:

    1847 The manuscript in the Pierpont Morgan Library
    1850 The text from *The Germ*
    1856 The text from *The Oxford and Cambridge Magazine*
    1869[1] The first Trial Book (before October 1869)
    1869[2] The second Trial Book (after October 1869)
    1870[a] The proof copy for *Poems* 1870
    1870 *Poems* (first edition)
    1870[2] *Poems* (second edition)
    1870[3] *Poems* (third edition)
    1870[4] *Poems* (fourth edition)
    1870[5] *Poems* (fifth edition), 1871
    1870[6] *Poems* (sixth edition), 1872
    1873 *Poems* (the Tauchnitz edition)
    1881 *Poems*, A New Edition

THE BLESSED DAMSEL

[i]   The blessed damsel leaned against
         The silver bar of Heaven.
     Her eyes knew more of rest and shade
         Than a deep water, even.
     She had three lilies in her hand
         And the stars in her hair were seven.

[ii] Her robe, ungirt from clasp to hem,
         No wrought flowers did adorn,
     But a white robe of Mary's gift
         For service meetly worn;
     And her hair lying down her back
         Was yellow like ripe corn.

[iii] Herseemed she scarce had been a day
         One of God's choristers;
     The wonder was not yet quite gone
         From that still look of hers;
     Albeit to them she left, her day
         Had counted as ten years.

[iv] (To *one* it is ten years of years.
         . . . . . Yet now, and in this place,
     Surely she leaned o'er me,—her hair
         Fell all about my face.
     Nothing: the autumn fall of leaves:
         The whole year sets apace.)

*THE
BLESSED
DAMSEL
1847*

[v] It was the rampart of God's house
    That she was standing on;
By God built over that sheer depth
    The which is Space begun;
So high, that looking downward thence,
    She scarce could see the sun.

[vii] Heard hardly, some of her new friends,
    Playing at holy games,
Spake gentle-mouthed among themselves
    Their virginal chaste names;
And the souls mounting up to God
    Went by her like thin flames.

[viii] And still she bowed herself & stooped
    Into the vast waste calm,
Till her bosom's pressure must have made
    The bar she leaned on warm,
And the lilies lay as if asleep
    Along her bended arm.

[ix] From the fixt lull of Heaven, she saw
    Time like a pulse shake fierce
Through all the worlds. Her gaze still strove
    Within that gulf to pierce
The swarm; and then she spake, as when
    The stars sang in their spheres.

[xii] "I wish that he were come to me,
    For he will come," she said.
"Have I not prayed in Heaven? on earth,
    Lord, Lord, has he not prayed?
Are not two prayers a perfect strength?
    And shall I feel afraid?

[xiii] "When round his head the aureole clings
  And he is clothed in white,
I'll take his hand and go with him
  To the deep wells of light,
And we will step down as to a stream
  And bathe there in God's sight.

[xiv] "We two will stand beside that shrine,
  Occult, withheld, untrod,
Whose lamps are stirred continually
  With prayers sent up to God;
And see our own prayers, granted, melt
  Each like a little cloud.

[xv] "We two will lie i' the shadow of
  That living mystic tree
Within whose secret growth the Dove
  Is sometimes felt to be,
While every leaf that His plumes touch
  Saith His name audibly.

[xvi] "And I myself will teach to him—
  I myself, lying so,—
The songs I sing here, which his voice
  Shall pause in, hushed & slow,
And find some knowledge at each pause,
  Or some new thing to know."

[xi] (Alas! just now, in that bird's song,
  Strove not her accents there
Fain to be hearkened? When those bells
  Possessed the midday air,
Was she not stepping to my side
  Upon a silver stair?)

THE BLESSED DAMSEL 1847

*THE
BLESSED
DAMSEL
1847*

[xviii] "We two," she said, "will seek the groves
　　　Where the lady Mary is,
　With her five handmaidens whose names
　　　Are five sweet symphonies;—
　Cecily, Gertrude, Magdalen,
　　　Margaret and Rosalys.

[xix] "They sit in circle, with bound locks
　　　And brows engarlanded;
　Into the fine cloth white like flame
　　　Weaving the golden thread
　To fashion the birth-robes for them
　　　Who are just born, being dead.

[xxi] "Herself shall bring us hand in hand
　　　To Him round whom all souls
　Kneel, the unnumbered ransomed heads
　　　Bowed with their aureoles;
　And Angels meeting us shall sing
　　　To their citherns and citoles.

[xxii] "There will I ask of Christ the Lord
　　　Thus much for him and me:—
　Only to live as once on earth
　　　At peace,—only to be
　As then awhile, for ever now
　　　Together, I and he."

[xxiii] She gazed and listened, and then said,
　　　Less sad of speech than mild:
　"All this is when he comes." She ceased:
　　　The light thrilled past her, filled
　With Angels in strong level lapse.
　　　Her eyes prayed, and she smiled.

[xxiv] (I saw her smile.) But soon their flight
        Was vague in distant spheres.
    And then she laid her arms along
        The shining barriers,
    And laid her face between her hands,
        And wept. (I heard her tears.)
            ——D. G. R. 1847

THE BLESSED DAMSEL 1847

THE BLESSED DAMOZEL

[i]   The blessed Damozel leaned out
      From the gold bar of Heaven:
  Her blue grave eyes were deeper much
      Than a deep water, even.
  She had three lilies in her hand,
      And the stars in her hair were seven.

[ii]   Her robe, ungirt from clasp to hem,
      No wrought flowers did adorn,
  But a white rose of Mary's gift
      On the neck meetly worn;
  And her hair, lying down her back,
      Was yellow like ripe corn.

[iii] Herseemed she scarce had been a day
      One of God's choristers;
  The wonder was not yet quite gone
      From that still look of hers;
  Albeit to them she left, her day
      Had counted as ten years.

[iv] (To *one* it is ten years of years:
      . . . . .Yet now, here in this place
  Surely she leaned o'er me,—her hair
      Fell all about my face. . . . .
  Nothing: the Autumn-fall of leaves.
      The whole year sets apace.)

*THE
BLESSED
DAMOZEL
1850*

[v] It was the terrace of God's house
    That she was standing on,—
By God build over the sheer depth
    In which Space is begun;
So high, that looking downward thence,
    She could scarce see the sun.

[vi] It lies from Heaven across the flood
    Of ether, as a bridge.
Beneath, the tides of day and night
    With flame and blackness ridge
The void, as low as where this earth
    Spins like a fretful midge.

[vi*a*] But in those tracts, with her, it was
    The peace of utter light
And silence. For no breeze may stir
    Along the steady flight
Of Seraphim; no echo there,
    Beyond all depth or height.

[vii] Heard hardly, some of her new friends,
    Playing at holy games,
Spake, gentle-mouthed, among themselves,
    Their virginal chaste names;
And the souls, mounting up to God,
    Went by her like thin flames.

[viii] And still she bowed herself, and stooped
    Into the vast waste calm;
Till her bosom's pressure must have made
    The bar she leaned on warm,
And the lilies lay as if asleep
    Along her bended arm.

[ix] From the fixt lull of heaven, she saw
　　　Time, like a pulse, shake fierce
　　Through all the worlds. Her gaze still strove,
　　　In that steep gulph, to pierce
　　The swarm: and then she spake, as when
　　　The stars sang in their spheres.

[xii] "I wish that he were come to me,
　　　For he will come," she said.
　　"Have I not prayed in solemn heaven?
　　　On earth, has he not prayed?
　　Are not two prayers a perfect strength?
　　　And shall I feel afraid?

[xiii] "When round his head the aureole clings,
　　　And he is clothed in white,
　　I'll take his hand, and go with him
　　　To the deep wells of light,
　　And we will step down as to a stream
　　　And bathe there in God's sight.

[xiv] "We two will stand beside that shrine,
　　　Occult, withheld, untrod,
　　Whose lamps tremble continually
　　　With prayer sent up to God;
　　And where each need, revealed, expects
　　　Its patient period.

[xv] "We two will lie i' the shadow of
　　　That living mystic tree
　　Within whose secret growth the Dove
　　　Sometimes is felt to be,
　　While every leaf that His plumes touch
　　　Saith His name audibly.

*THE
BLESSED
DAMOZEL
1850*

*THE
BLESSED
DAMOZEL
1850*

[xvi] "And I myself will teach to him—
　　I myself, lying so,—
　The songs I sing here; which his mouth
　　Shall pause in, hushed and slow,
　Finding some knowledge at each pause
　　And some new thing to know."

[xvi*a*] (Alas! to *her* wise simple mind
　　These things were all but known
　Before: they trembled on her sense,—
　　Her voice had caught their tone.
　Alas for lonely Heaven! Alas
　　For life wrung out alone!

[xvi*b*] Alas, and though the end were reached? . . . .
　　Was *thy* part understood
　Or borne in trust? And for her sake
　　Shall this too be found good?—
　May the close lips that knew not prayer
　　Praise ever, though they would?)

[xviii] "We two," she said, "will seek the groves
　　Where the lady Mary is,
　With her five handmaidens, whose names
　　Are five sweet symphonies:—
　Cecily, Gertrude, Magdalen,
　　Margaret, and Rosalys.

[xix] "Circle-wise sit they, with bound locks
　　And bosoms covered;
　Into the fine cloth, white like flame,
　　Weaving the golden thread,
　To fashion the birth-robes for them
　　Who are just born, being dead.

[xx] "He shall fear haply, and be dumb.
    Then I will lay my cheek
To his, and tell about our love,
    Not once abashed or weak:
And the dear Mother will approve
    My pride, and let me speak.

[xxi] "Herself shall bring us, hand in hand,
    To Him round whom all souls
Kneel—the unnumber'd solemn heads
    Bowed with their aureoles:
And Angels, meeting us, shall sing
    To their citherns and citoles.

[xxii] "There will I ask of Christ the Lord
    Thus much for him and me:—
To have more blessing than on earth
    In no wise; but to be
As then we were,—being as then
    At peace. Yea, verily.

[xxii*a*] "Yea, verily; when he is come
    We will do thus and thus:
Till this my vigil seems quite strange
    And almost fabulous;
We two will live at once, one life;
    And peace shall be with us."

[xxiii] She gazed, and listened, and then said,
    Less sad of speech than mild:
"All this is when he comes." She ceased;
    The light thrilled past her, filled
With Angels, in strong level lapse.
    Her eyes prayed, and she smiled.

THE BLESSED DAMOZEL 1850

THE BLESSED DAMOZEL 1850

[xxiv] (I saw her smile.) But soon their flight
        Was vague 'mid the poised spheres.
    And then she cast her arms along
        The golden barriers,
    And laid her face between her hands,
        And wept. (I heard her tears.)

THE BLESSED DAMOZEL

---

[i]   The blessed Damozel lean'd out
      From the gold bar of Heaven;
  Her eyes knew more of rest and shade
      Than waters still'd at even;
  She had three lilies in her hand,
      And the stars in her hair were seven.

[ii]   Her robe, ungirt from clasp to hem,
      No wrought flowers did adorn,
  But a white rose of Mary's gift,
      For service meetly worn;
  And her hair lying down her back
      Was yellow like ripe corn.

[iii]   Her seem'd she scarce had been a day
      One of God's choristers;
  The wonder was not yet quite gone
      From that still look of hers;
  Albeit, to them she left, her day
      Had counted as ten years.

[iv]   (To *one*, it is ten years of years.
      . . . . Yet now, and in this place,
  Surely she lean'd o'er me—her hair
      Fell all about my face. . . . . . .
  Nothing: the autumn fall of leaves.
      The whole year sets apace.)

THE
BLESSED
DAMOZEL
1856

[v] It was the rampart of God's house
  That she was standing on;
By God built over the sheer depth
  The which is Space begun;
So high, that looking downward thence
  She scarce could see the sun.

[vi] It lies in Heaven, across the flood
  Of ether, as a bridge.
Beneath, the tides of day and night
  With flame and blackness ridge
The void, as low as where this earth
  Spins like a fretful midge.

[vii] She scarcely heard her sweet new friends:
  Playing at holy games,
Softly they spake among themselves
  Their virginal chaste names;
And the souls, mounting up to God,
  Went by her like thin flames.

[viii] And still she bow'd above the vast
  Waste sea of worlds that swarm;
Until her bosom must have made
  The bar she lean'd on warm,
And the lilies lay as if asleep
  Along her bended arm.

[ix] From the fix'd place of Heaven, she saw
  Time like a pulse shake fierce
Through all the worlds. Her gaze still strove
  Within the gulf to pierce
Its path; and now she spoke, as when
  The stars sung in their spheres.

THE
BLESSED
DAMOZEL
1856

[x] The sun was gone now. The curl'd moon
　　　　Was like a little feather
　　Fluttering far down the gulf. And now
　　　　She spoke through the still weather.
　　Her voice was like the voice the stars
　　　　Had when they sung together.

[xii] "I wish that he were come to me,
　　　　For he will come," she said.
　　"Have I not pray'd in Heaven?—on earth,
　　　　Lord, Lord, has he not pray'd?
　　Are not two prayers a perfect strength?
　　　　And shall I feel afraid?

[xiii] "When round his head the aureole clings,
　　　　And he is clothed in white,
　　I'll take his hand and go with him
　　　　To the deep wells of light,
　　And we will step down as to a stream,
　　　　And bathe there in God's sight.

[xiv] "We two will stand beside that shrine,
　　　　Occult, withheld, untrod,
　　Whose lamps are stirr'd continually
　　　　With prayers sent up to God;
　　And see our old prayers, granted, melt
　　　　Each like a little cloud.

[xv] "We two will lie i' the shadow of
　　　　That living mystic tree,
　　Within whose secret growth the Dove
　　　　Is sometimes felt to be,
　　While every leaf that His plumes touch
　　　　Saith His Name audibly.

*THE
BLESSED
DAMOZEL
1856*

[xvi] "And I myself will teach to him,
    I myself, lying so,
The songs I sing here; which his voice
    Shall pause in, hush'd and slow,
And find some knowledge at each pause,
    Or some new thing to know."

[xi] (Ah sweet! Just now, in that bird's song,
    Strove not her accents there
Fain to be hearken'd? When those bells
    Possess'd the midday air,
Was she not stepping to my side
    Down all the trembling stair?)

[xviii] "We two," she said, "will seek the groves
    Where the Lady Mary is,
With her five handmaidens, whose names
    Are five sweet symphonies,
Cecily, Gertrude, Magdalen,
    Margaret, and Rosalys.

[xix] "Circlewise sit they, with bound locks
    And foreheads garlanded;
Into the fine cloth white like flame
    Weaving the golden thread,
To fashion the birth-robes for them
    Who are just born, being dead.

[xx] "He shall fear, haply, and be dumb;
    Then I will lay my cheek
To his, and tell about our love,
    Not once abash'd or weak:
And the dear Mother will approve
    My pride, and let me speak.

THE
BLESSED
DAMOZEL
1856

[xxi] "Herself shall bring us, hand in hand,
  To Him round whom all souls
 Kneel, the unnumber'd ransom'd heads
  Bow'd with their aureoles:
And angels meeting us shall sing
  To their citherns and citoles.

[xxii] "There will I ask of Christ the Lord
  Thus much for him and me:—
 Only to live as once on earth
  At peace—only to be
As then awhile, for ever now
  Together, I and he."

[xxiii] She gazed, and listen'd, and then said,
  Less sad of speech than mild,
 "All this is when he comes." She ceased.
  The light thrill'd past her, fill'd
With angels in strong level lapse.
  Her eyes pray'd, and she smiled.

[xxiv] (I saw her smile.) But soon their flight
  Was vague in distant spheres;
 And then she laid her arms along
  The golden barriers,
And laid her face between her hands,
  And wept. (I heard her tears.)

THE BLESSED DAMOZEL

[i]   The blessed damozel leaned out
      From the gold bar of Heaven;
  Her eyes were deeper than the depth
      Of waters stilled at even;
  She had three lilies in her hand,   5
      And the stars in her hair were seven.

[ii]   Her robe, ungirt from clasp to hem,
      No wrought flowers did adorn,
  But a white rose of Mary's gift,
      For service meetly worn;   10
  Her hair that lay along her back
      Was yellow like ripe corn.

[iii]   Herseemed she scarce had been a day
      One of God's choristers;
  The wonder was not yet quite gone   15
      From that still look of hers;
  Albeit, to them she left, her day
      Had counted as ten years.

---

[i]	[ii]

1-4 The blessed damsel leaned against
     The silver bar of Heaven.
     Her eyes knew more of rest and shade
     Than a deep water, even. 1847
	9 rose] robe 1847
	10 On the neck meetly worn 1850
	11 And her hair lying down her back
	                            1847-1869[2]

3-4 Her blue grave eyes were deeper much
     Than a deep water, even. 1850
     Her eyes knew more of rest and shade
     Than waters still'd at even; 1856
	[iii]
	13 Her seem'd 1856

*THE
BLESSED
DAMOZEL
1881*

[iv]   (To one, it is ten years of years.
    . . . Yet now, and in this place,   20
  Surely she leaned o'er me—her hair
    Fell all about my face. . . .
  Nothing: the autumn-fall of leaves.
    The whole year sets apace.)

[v]   It was the rampart of God's house   25
    That she was standing on;
  By God built over the sheer depth
    The which is Space begun;
  So high, that looking downward thence
    She scarce could see the sun.   30

[vi]   It lies in Heaven, across the flood
    Of ether, as a bridge.
  Beneath, the tides of day and night
    With flame and darkness ridge
  The void, as low as where this earth   35
    Spins like a fretful midge.

[iv]
Whole stanza in italics 1869¹-1870²
19 *one* 1847-1856
20 and] here 1850
23 autumn-fall] autumn fall 1847, 1856, 1870-1873; Autumn-fall 1850

[v]
25 rampart] terrace 1850
27 the] that 1847
28 In which Space is begun 1850
30 scarce could] could scarce 1850

[vi]
om. 1847; first in 1850
31 in] from 1850
34 darkness] blackness 1850, 1856

[vi*a*]
Between 36 and 37 1850 had the **stanza**, afterwards cancelled:

  But in those tracts, with her, it was
    The peace of utter light
  And silence. For no breeze may stir
    Along the steady flight
  Of Seraphim; no echo there,
    Beyond all depth or height.

[vii] Around her, lovers, newly met
         'Mid deathless love's acclaims,
     Spoke evermore among themselves
         Their heart-remembered names;   40
     And the souls mounting up to God
         Went by her like thin flames.

[viii] And still she bowed herself and stooped
         Out of the circling charm;
     Until her bosom must have made   45
         The bar she leaned on warm,
     And the lilies lay as if asleep
         Along her bended arm.

THE
BLESSED
DAMOZEL
1881

[vii]
37 Heard hardly, some of her new friends, 1847, 1850, 1869,² 1870¹-1870⁶
   She scarcely heard her sweet new friends: 1856, 1869¹
38 Playing at holy games, 1847-1856
   Amid their loving games 1869¹-1870⁶
   In joy no sorrow claims 1872
39 Spake gentle-mouthed among themselves 1847
   Spake, gentle-mouthed, among themselves 1850
   Softly they spake among themselves 1856, 1869¹
   Spake evermore among themselves 1869²-1870⁵
   Spoke evermore among themselves 1870⁶-1881
40 Their virginal chaste names; 1847-1870⁶
   Their rapturous new names 1872, 1873

[viii]
43 And still she bowed herself & stooped 1847
   And still she bowed herself, and stooped 1850
   And still she bow'd above the vast 1856-1869²
44 Into the vast waste calm 1847, 1850
   Waste sea of worlds that swarm 1856-1869²
45 Till her bosom's pressure must have made 1847, 1850

*THE
BLESSED
DAMOZEL
1881*

[ix] From the fixed place of Heaven she saw
  Time like a pulse shake fierce 50
Through all the worlds. Her gaze still strove
  Within the gulf to pierce
Its path; and now she spoke as when
  The stars sang in their spheres.

[x] The sun was gone now; the curled moon 55
  Was like a little feather
Fluttering far down the gulf; and now
  She spoke through the still weather.
Her voice was like the voice the stars
  Had when they sang together. 60

[xi] (Ah sweet! Even now, in that bird's song,
  Strove not her accents there,
Fain to be hearkened? When those bells
  Possessed the mid-day air,
Strove not her steps to reach my side 65
  Down all the echoing stair?)

[ix]
49 place] lull 1847, 1850
52 Within the gulf] Within that gulf 1847; In that steep gulph 1850
53 The swarm; and then she spake, as when 1847
The swarm: and then she spake, as when 1850
54 sang] sung 1856

[x]
om. 1847, 1850
60 sang] sung 1856

[xi]
stood between 96 and 97 in 1847, 1856-1870[a]; om. 1850; printed in italics 1869[1]-1870[a]
61 Alas! just now, 1847; Ah sweet! Just now, 1856-1870[a]
64 mid-day] midday 1847, 1856
66 Upon a silver stair? 1847
Down all the trembling stair? 1856-1870[a]

[26]

[xii] 'I wish that he were come to me,
  For he will come,' she said.
 'Have I not prayed in Heaven?—on earth,
  Lord, Lord, has he not pray'd? 70
 Are not two prayers a perfect strength?
  And shall I feel afraid?

[xiii] 'When round his head the aureole clings,
  And he is clothed in white,
 I'll take his hand and go with him 75
  To the deep wells of light;
 As unto a stream we will step down,
  And bathe there in God's sight.

[xiv] 'We two will stand beside that shrine,
  Occult, withheld, untrod, 80
 Whose lamps are stirred continually
  With prayer sent up to God;
 And see our old prayers, granted, melt
  Each like a little cloud.

THE
BLESSED
DAMOZEL
1881

[xii]
69 in Heaven?—on earth] in solemn
  heaven? 1850
70 Lord, Lord,] On earth, 1850
[xiii]
77 And we will step down as to a stream
  1847-1856
 We will step down as to a stream
  1869¹-1873

[xiv]
81 are stirred] tremble 1850
82 prayer] prayers 1847, 1856
83 old] own 1847
83-84 And where each need, revealed,
    expects
  Its patient period. 1850

*THE
BLESSED
DAMOZEL
1881*

[xv] 'We two will lie i' the shadow of   85
    That living mystic tree
Within whose secret growth the Dove
    Is sometimes felt to be,
While every leaf that His plumes touch
    Saith His Name audibly.   90

[xvi] 'And I myself will teach to him,
    I myself, lying so,
The songs I sing here; which his voice
    Shall pause in, hushed and slow,
And find some knowledge at each pause,   95
    Or some new thing to know.'

[xvii] (Alas! We two, we two, thou say'st!
    Yea, one wast thou with me
That once of old. But shall God lift
    To endless unity   100
The soul whose likeness with thy soul
    Was but its love for thee?)

[xv]
88 Is sometimes] Sometimes is 1850

[xvi]
93 voice] mouth 1850
95 And find] Finding 1850
96 Or] And 1850

[xvii]
om. 1847-1870ª; but these (except 1850) had xi here; 1850 here had two stanzas, afterwards cancelled:

[xvii*a*]
(Alas! to *her* wise simple mind
  These things were all but known
Before: they trembled on her sense,—
  Her voice had caught their tone.
Alas for lonely Heaven! Alas
  For life wrung out alone!

[xvii*b*]
Alas, and though the end were reached?
   . . . .
  Was *thy* part understood
Or borne in trust? And for her sake
  Shall this too be found good?—
May the close lips that knew not prayer
  Praise ever, though they would?)

THE
BLESSED
DAMOZEL
1881

[xviii] 'We two,' she said, 'will seek the groves
　　　　　Where the lady Mary is,
　　　With her five handmaidens, whose names　105
　　　　　Are five sweet symphonies,
　　　Cecily, Gertrude, Magdalen,
　　　　　Margaret and Rosalys.

[xix] 'Circlewise sit they, with bound locks
　　　　　And foreheads garlanded;　110
　　　Into the fine cloth white like flame
　　　　　Weaving the golden thread,
　　　To fashion the birth-robes for them
　　　　　Who are just born, being dead.

[xx] 'He shall fear, haply, and be dumb:　115
　　　　　Then will I lay my cheek
　　　To his, and tell about our love,
　　　　　Not once abashed or weak:
　　　And the dear Mother will approve
　　　　　My pride, and let me speak.　120

[xxi] 'Herself shall bring us, hand in hand,
　　　　　To Him round whom all souls
　　　Kneel, the clear-ranged unnumbered heads
　　　　　Bowed with their aureoles:
　　　And angels meeting us shall sing　125
　　　　　To their citherns and citoles.

　　　　　　[xix]
109- They sit in circle, with bound locks
110　And brows engarlanded; 1847
　　　Circle-wise sit they, with bound locks
　　　And bosoms covered; 1850
　　　　　　[xx]
om. 1847
116　will I] I will 1850, 1856

　　　　　　[xxi]
125　Kneel, the unnumbered ransomed
　　　　　　　　　　heads 1847
　　　Kneel—the unnumber'd solemn heads
　　　　　　　　　　1850
　　　Kneel, the unnumber'd ransom'd
　　　　　　　　　　heads 1856

*THE
BLESSED
DAMOZEL
1881*

[xxii] 'There will I ask of Christ the Lord
    Thus much for him and me:—
Only to live as once on earth
    With Love,—only to be,   130
As then awhile, for ever now
    Together, I and he.'

[xxiii] She gazed and listened and then said,
    Less sad of speech than mild,—
'All this is when he comes.' She ceased   135
    The light thrilled towards her, fill'd
With angels in strong level flight.
    Her eyes prayed, and she smil'd.

[xxiv] (I saw her smile.) But soon their path
    Was vague in distant spheres: 140
And then she cast her arms along
    The golden barriers,
And laid her face between her hands,
    And wept. (I heard her tears.)

[xxii]
129 To have more blessing than on earth 1850
130 At peace,—only to be 1847, 1856
    In nowise; but to be 1850
131 As then we were,—being as then 1850
132 At peace. Yea, verily. 1850
Between 132 and 133 1850 had a stanza, afterwards cancelled:

[xxii*b*]
"Yea, verily; when he is come
    We will do thus and thus:
Till this my vigil seem quite strange
    And almost fabulous;
We two will live at once, one life;
    And peace shall be with us."

[xxiii]
136 towards] past 1847-1856
137 flight] lapse 1847-1856

[xxiv]
139 (I . . . smile.) in italics 1869^1-1870^a; path] flight 1847-1856
140 in distant] 'mid the poised 1850
141 cast] laid 1847, 1856
142 golden] shining 1847
144 (I . . . tears.) in italics 1869^1-1870^a

www.ingramcontent.com/pod-product-compliance
Lightning Source LLC
Chambersburg PA
CBHW080740230426
43665CB00020B/2802